12/10

W9-AUA-527

Peter,

I hope you enjoy
reading
New York, New York
as much as you like
living here.

Best wishes

R. Sh

New York, New York
So Good They Named It Twice

An Irreverant Guide to Experiencing and
Living in the Greatest City in the World

by Rob Silverman

BROADFIELD BOOKS

Acknowledgments

I have to thank Janet Silverman, Jonah Silverman and Marlee Silverman. And a special mention for Betsy Thorpe.

To Bradley Silverman and Dana Silverman

Contents

Introduction   ix

Part 1: Your Home in the City

Chapter 1: Renting an Apartment   3
Chapter 2: Co-ops, Condos, and the Buying Process   9
Chapter 3: Doormen   14
Chapter 4: Superintendents   20
Chapter 5: Tipping for the Holidays   26
Chapter 6: Neighborhood Pride   30

Part 2: Transportation

Chapter 7: New York Has a Monorail?   39
Chapter 8: Taxi!   44
Chapter 9: Car Services   55
Chapter 10: Owning and Parking a Car in the City   59
Chapter 11: Driving and Traffic Tips   65
Chapter 12: Public Transportation   73
Chapter 13: Life as a Pedestrian   86

Part 3: Raising Kids and Pets in the City

Chapter 14: Manhattan Kids   95

Chapter 15: The Manhattan Nanny   100
Chapter 16: The Private School Admissions Process   107
Chapter 17: How Much for Tuition?   120
Chapter 18: Dogs and Their Owners   125

Part 4: Restaurants and Entertainment

Chapter 19: Ordering My First New York Sandwich   135
Chapter 20: Restaurants and Reservations   143
Chapter 21: Manhattan Movie Etiquette   160
Chapter 22: Shops and Shopping   168
Chapter 23: A Manhattan Calendar Year   172

Part 5: Living in the City

Chapter 24: Making Friends in the Manhattan   179
Chapter 25: The Weather   185
Chapter 26: 9/11 and Life after It   190
Chapter 27: The Two Blackouts   193
Chapter 28: Hatch, Match, and Dispatch   199
Chapter 29: The Rich, the Poor, and Everyone Else   208
Chapter 30: Where Are You From?   220

Introduction

Manhattan has a nighttime population of fewer than two million people. While it is only one of the five boroughs that make up New York City, but with apologies to all the residents of the other four, Manhattan is the borough most associated with visions of New York City. Manhattan is a noncolossal 23 square miles in area. It is just over 13 miles long and never reaches 2.5 miles wide. It is the most densely populated county in the whole of the United States, with over seventy-one thousand people per square mile. But such is the astonishing anonymity of this amazing city that I know no one who lives on my apartment floor by name, and do not even know who lies behind three of the apartment doors located at the other end of the hall, having never seen them open or close.

The daytime Manhattan population is a completely different story, doubling, and in holiday periods triples in size and complexity. The pace of life here is so fast that you think you are crawling wherever else you travel to in the world.

This book is not about the beautiful architecture of the city, nor is it about the history of the people who live or work here. New York City, and in particular Manhattan, is so unique that it generates its own culture, its own attitude, and its own exclusiveness. These attributes bring with them tons of idiosyncrasies and quirks that need to be explored and commented on to truly understand what it is like to live, breathe, work, and play here. It's what makes New York, New York so good they named it twice.

After living in New York City for over half of my adult life, I still find myself in many New York moments that remind me why I'm living in the greatest city in the world. Strolling in Central Park in the summer with my kids, we might come across an impromptu roller-skating ballet, while in the winter, the park is chockablock full of kids pulling sleds to capture the best of a snowy day. There are situations and events that are exclusive to the tiny island of Manhattan: cheering on the thousands of participants in the New York City Marathon; passing by the Puerto Rican day parade on Fifth Avenue, complete with tank-topped men bearing pythons wrapped around their shoulders; trying to get past the mad rush in Times Square at 8:00 p.m. when all the theatres on Broadway are about to start. Times like these help engender the phrase "Only in New York."

Even after living here for twenty years, walking down the avenues I will still stare up at the skyscrapers, in awe of their beauty. I'm continually finding myself overwhelmed by the incredible choice of restaurants, the convenience of having so many amenities right at my fingertips. I love living here. I work here, eat here, sleep here, am raising my children here, play here, and most likely will die here. Everything I need to live a happy and complete life is right on my doorstep. I could spend the rest of my life in New York City without ever leaving. The only thing I can't do here is get buried, because there is no space for dead bodies. So inevitably I will eternally end up somewhere else, but until that day I will be in Manhattan.

This book describes every aspect of being in this tremendous city: ordering at a deli, the delights of shopping its famous stores, negotiating the subways and buses, walking across its streets, deciding to rent or buy an apartment, hiring nannies, and finding doctors. I discuss what times taxicabs change their shifts and how it affects your ability to get a cab on a rainy night, and debate the desirability of making eye contact in the subway system.

On many occasions, I relate stories from my own life to give the content depth and humor. I have experienced so much here—a dash to secure a private room for my wife minutes after the births of my children, participating in some Rocky feel-good moments at a Times Square movie theatre, unknowingly insulting our babysitter, agonizing over tips to the large staff at our apartment building, trying to cross from the East Side to the West on a parade day, and after a trip or two to the suburbs, vowing never to spend an overnight visit there.

Ever wonder why co-ops are less expensive than condos? Learn why you should always keep the superintendent of your building happy, and what is and is not acceptable behavior at movie theatres (yes, talking back to the characters on the screen is de rigueur). Being a part of this city, whether one is born here or moved here later in life, can be described only in these thousands of moments. Nothing else gives a resident or visitor a sense of what it is like to be here than to describe everyday occurrences that express the pace, vibe, and feel of New York City.

This book is about the who, what, and why that make this city tick, coupled with humorous observations, stories, and straightforward advice to make living in the greatest city in the world the greatest experience for all.

New York, New York

PART 1

Your Home in the City

CHAPTER 1

Renting an Apartment

Most newcomers and many old-timers rent rather than buy an apartment in the city. The phenomenon of renting a home stems from the high price of buying a place in Manhattan and the large deposits needed to get a mortgage and get board approval after the subprime mortgage collapse. In times of uncertainty and lack of a guarantee of property appreciation, more and more inhabitants of Manhattan choose to rent. It takes less time to rent an apartment than buy one; the checks landlords carry out on tenants are not as severe as those that co-op boards and banks insist on. It is also far easier to terminate a lease through nonrenewal or breakage, as opposed to trying to sell an apartment. Finally, the closing costs of buying and selling far outweigh the closing costs of renting, where a rental fee charged by a broker may or may not be applicable.

The traditional way of renting an apartment is fast disappearing. The old-fashioned way is that the prospective renter finds a broker, usually affiliated with a large real estate brokerage company in Manhattan. You fill out a form that covers how much you want to spend, where you want to live, how many square feet and number of bedrooms you want, who you may be sharing the apartment with, if you have a burning desire to own a dog, what amenities you are looking for, and so on. Once the form has been filled in and reviewed by the broker, you trudge around the city viewing apartments that have very little in common with the answers to the questionnaire you have filled in. What you will be shown are apartments that are available or soon will be. If you want to live on the Upper East Side, don't be surprised to be shown apartments in Murray Hill with an explanation that it is only a short subway ride from the Upper East Side. If you want two bedrooms, you will be shown "junior fours": a term made up to explain one bedroom, one living room, one bathroom, and a closet for the second bedroom, which magically appears from an alcove in the living room with a moveable wall.

Searching for an apartment in this way can be very frustrating, but understand that brokers can only show you what they have, and at buoyant times in the economy there is a shortage in supply of rentable apartments. During economic downturns, the true nature of transient Manhattan life is reflected in the high turnover of Manhattan apartments. As households cut costs, many realize that the best way is to reduce the amount spent on rent. Hoards of frugal-minded folk vacate to the outer boroughs, the suburbs, and out of state in order to save money. The effect on apartment rentals from economic woes is pretty severe, and those who have disposable income can get some great bargains in finding apartments when this occurs. Fees disappear, the cost of high-end rentals comes down quite considerably, and for each dollar spent more amenities are thrown in. Just to rent the vacant apartments for a year, some landlords offer a couple of months rent free and pay the broker themselves, shifting the burden away from the tenant.

The modern way of trying to rent an apartment in Manhattan involves very little trudging around the city. Instead, most of the groundwork is done in front of a computer screen. Numerous Web sites that focus on bridging the gap between a landlord and renter have popped up in the last decade. Filters exist, narrowing down searches to exact neighborhoods and apartment specifications. This has replaced the broker as the most popular method of finding an apartment. As a result, finding a rental has become for the most part fee free, much easier to hone in on prerequisites and generally more of an enjoyable process. With the use of photos online and sometimes videos, it is possible to make a decision without even visiting the apartment. It is what the computer was invented for: to make life more convenient for the consumer as well as creating the largest marketplace for those who have products to sell.

The degree of quality control and vetting of prospective tenants depends upon the type of building and quantity of rent to be paid. The landlord will need verification of employment from your immediate boss. They will need recent bank statements showing that you are not heavily overdrawn. Tenants will need sound credit reports, the benchmark of how many points you will require may vary from landlord to landlord. Any unpaid bills, no matter how small, from previous rentals can come back and bite you quite hard with an application rejected. The key is to have your records in good working order corroborated by some glowing references to ensure a successful pursuit of a rental. Fabricating a rental contract backed up with false references and nonexistent employers can lead to problems even after taking possession of the rental. My late grandmother always said that "lies have feet," and they tend to walk in on you when you feel most comfortable and when you no longer remember what the truth is. Honesty is always the best policy.

The memories of the Great Depression and the effort common folk put into the war effort in the '40s have lingered in the treatment of tenants in the city. Landlords do face difficulty in evicting tenants even in some of the most extreme cases, and more often than not the courts can take months to sort out the backlog of cases and bring new ones to trial. Let it be known that nonpayment of rent is a serious breach of contract and will eventually be dealt with by the landlord directly or the courts. Your credit score will be ruined, you will have to move back in with your family as rent default tends to be off-putting to future landlords, and during your standoff with the landlord you may want to look over your shoulder a couple of times when walking down the street.

Once in an apartment, it is important to remember that you don't actually own the apartment and that any changes you want to make to the floor plan need approval of the landlord and in turn the board of the building if it is a co-op or a condo. Even the best do-it-yourself enthusiasts should not embark on subdividing rooms, adding outside space, or redesigning the bathrooms. Similarly, if the rental agreement is in your name only, by all means have guests over to stay, but don't start operating a bed-and-breakfast facility charging them nightly rates. Subletting of an apartment is feasible, providing the landlord gives approval. If he doesn't, then charging someone else rent and making a profit out of your rental apartment is really stealing money from the landlord.

What makes New York City unique is the existence of the strangely outdated rent control and rent stabilization laws. They were implemented with the aim of providing affordable housing to a large segment of the population, thus maintaining the mixed social fabric of the city. Manhattan shouldn't be just for the rich. The problem is that these laws are exploited by the tenant, as there are strict conditions under which a controlled or subsidized apartment can be rented. The pool of these types of apartments is shrinking fast as the city failed to add new sources of supply since the programs' beginnings. The main ingredients for qualification include an ability to pay based on income, if you are a close relative to someone already in the apartment and you live with them, and that it is your primary residence with no subletting.

It is amazing how many friends I know who supposedly live with Granny, earn $12,000 a year, and live on the fourth floor of a walk-up in the Village. In reality they live in New Jersey with their wife and two kids, drive a Mercedes sedan, and buried the grandmother twelve years ago. If you ever visit the rent-controlled apartment that leases for $150 a month and is sublet for $1,500 a month, you will meet three very nice New York University students, oblivious to any New York City regulations, who have converted a one bedroom into a three bedroom, all inside a 450-square-foot apartment.

Therefore, New York City housing remains somewhat affordable to those less fortunate and less well-off, not because of the laws designed to protect them but by the pursuit of profit from those who flagrantly abuse them.

CHAPTER 2

Co-ops, Condos, and the Buying Process

Condos in Manhattan cost more than co-cops, because when you buy the apartment you actually own the unit and can sell it without board approval. Whereas, when you buy a co-op, the building is owned and managed by a corporation in which shares are sold to the owners, allowing them to occupy individual units. So with a co-op, you sort of own the apartment but not really because a co-op board can stop you from buying and selling it. Millions of New Yorkers since the beginning of the last century have bought property they don't really own and sold it to other nonowners. In reality the co-op system works so long as boards operate in the best interest of the entire apartment building and employ a competent management company. Confusing isn't it?

Most apartment owners buy co-ops because they are cheaper and because they are in greater supply. The main drawback to buying a co-op is that the co-op board sets an exact percentage that an owner has to put down as a deposit on the apartment. This starts at 20 percent and rises to as much as 60 percent in the more paranoid and financially frugal buildings. You can't borrow this money, and the buyer has to provide the money trail for the purchase to be board approved. Unlike with a condo, co-op buyers have to present to the board an entire financial statement showing that they can afford to purchase the apartment and then pay the mortgage and common charges, and that each future co-op tenant is a good fit with the rest of the building.

In order to ascertain who is in and who is out, a prospective buyer has first to agree to a price with the seller, usually through real estate agents, as is the case with all real estate transactions. A co-op purchaser then has to fill out a questionnaire listing his assets and liabilities with copies of bank statements, proof of stock ownership, copies of an approved mortgage, and even copies of divorce papers showing alimony and child support payments. Let it be known that when you buy a co-op apartment in Manhattan, every member of the board will know every little detail of your financial life, and by the time they have told their friends and neighbors, the entire building will know you intimately and probably will be giving you funny looks. The best advice is to put down as much as you need to qualify for the purchase with a little cushion on top, but there is no reason to list every asset that you own because there is nothing worse than being the wealthiest person in a building on paper if everyone in that building knows it.

Candidates for a co-op are interviewed, and their files are distributed to all the members of the board in advance of the interview as well as to the managing agent. The interview is normally held in one of the board members' apartments after work during the week. The board meets normally once a month, unless it's in the summer when they never meet. So if you agree to a price in May, don't even think about being brought before the board until early September after Labor Day.

The composition of the board varies from building to building and neighborhood to neighborhood. Being a board member is a huge responsibility and takes up a considerable amount of time. Elections are held yearly to all the positions on the board from president to secretary to treasurer to general member, and most candidates do need to campaign yearly. There are usually three types of people who sit on a board: If you own a large unit the best way of protecting your asset is to sit on the board and try to keep the costs of running the building at a minimum while preserving value and services. The second is, if you are thinking of selling your unit in the not-too-distant future. Sitting on the board means you get to vote for a prospective buyer of your own unit and all objections to the new owner have to be voiced to your face. It makes for interesting board meetings. The third type of board member is someone who has absolutely nothing better to do than sit on a board made up of other self-interested megalomaniacs. These folk are normally slightly older, often retirees, who are in search of companionship and finding out and spreading idle gossip in the building and enjoy sorting through mounds of bureaucracy.

Very few of these board members would be used

for PR purposes for trying to entice would-be buyers. After the interview the most common thought in the buyer's mind is: "Why am I buying into this building?" The questions in the interview are always contrived and bear little relevance to whether the buyer is qualified or not to live in the building. All the answers to the questions are found in the paperwork that the buyer has already filled out and handed in weeks previously. As long as the buyer remains even-keeled and answers the questions politely, and the answers are truthful and not fabricated so that Pinocchio looks honest in comparison, then the interview is more rubber-stamping than selective.

Moving into an apartment and doing renovations is a whole different ball game, and tests the most patient of owners. Board members have an underlying need to see an apartment sold simply to maintain, if not increase, the value of their own. What they don't like is noisy neighbors clogging up elevators, smashing the lobby while moving heavy furniture, and the hiring of clumsy removal men who show little regard for anyone's property rights. The move in normally is completed in one day and coordination between superintendents, tenants, doormen, and the managing agent ensures that it all runs smoothly, providing the right palms have been greased. It's amazing in New York how quickly things move along when the right point people are "taken care of."

The move in is usually the end of an arduous task of finding a new place to rest one's head at night. Before the big day approaches, at a bare minimum the walls of the new abode would need to be painted. Everything in a co-op needs approval from the board. Therefore, it is always advisable to be on good terms with board members whenever work needs to be done in your apartment. Every rejection costs YOU time and most of all money, as new applications and revised plans always carry a fee if not fees. It is highly recommended that you use a contractor who has already done work in the building since the board would be familiar with him and the process will move quicker. The one thing you really want to avoid is moving into the apartment before the work has been completed. Living in a construction site involves large amounts of dust, strange men who speak no English turning up at your door at 9:00 a.m., lots of empty soda cans appearing on window ledges, music blaring at all times from transistor radios, large discolored sheets covering items of furniture, and stray ladders that rise from the ground and serve no other purpose than clutter. Most importantly you never want to be at home when neighbors and board members show up to complain about all of the above.

CHAPTER 3

Doormen

Having somebody open a door for you every time you enter or leave your apartment building is nice, but does not really factor into a defining moment in one's daily life. Most of those who get out of bed each morning and go to work are able to open a door by themselves. Living in a doorman building is prestigious, and doorman-building inhabitants tend to turn their nose up at nondoormen walk-up folk. The role of a doorman in this respect goes far beyond opening a door.

They are first and foremost a deterrent against crime. The theory is that they are a line of defense against prospective burglars and kidnappers, and women particularly prefer living in doorman buildings because sex crimes do occur more often than not in walk-ups at the moment of entry into the building. Anyone who enters a doorman building is scrutinized as to why he is there, and who he has come to see. If the tenant is not in, guests cannot use the elevator and gain entry into an apartment, even if they are in possession of a key, but instead must remain in the lobby with the doorman, if they choose, until the tenant returns to accompany them. Unless a signed letter is received by the doorman from the tenant explaining who, why, and how long a guest will be staying with them, entry is also refused. Every detail is written down about guests who are allowed access to an apartment and is kept in a book or computer at the front desk. Guests, unless recognized, always have to show identification. A tenant really does feel secure with a doorman at the front of the building. Without the worry of being burgled and pillaged in your own home by gangs of disgruntled youth, the tenant can free up his thoughts on more productive matters.

Sorry to disappoint many of you out there, but a solitary unarmed doorman in a sleepy small building on a side street shrouded with trees can't really do much to prevent a full-scale onslaught by those who are determined to do harm to people and property. Some doorman buildings have more cameras than a photo shop but so do banks and they get held up frequently.

Doormen are therefore a deterrent to unwanted guests. They offer peace of mind to the tenant. They are not security guards, so if you have the Russian mafia hounding you for nonpayment of a loan you should not expect a Manhattan doorman to take out and neutralize a bunch of club-wielding thugs whose sole purpose is to damage your kneecaps as a reminder of payment due.

Doormen make life easier for the tenant. They take and record all deliveries and handle anything that needs shipping out of the lobby to the outside world. All clean clothes returning from a two-day excursion to the neighborhood dry cleaner end up being accepted and stored by the doorman awaiting your arrival home. Any visit to a supermarket from which your purchases were deemed too heavy to carry will pass through your doorman either sent up in the building's trolley by elevator or by the delivery person themselves supervised by the doorman. Everything that the doorman does at work on a daily basis is for the convenience of the tenant.

Never fear about not being home for delivery of a package, no matter how urgent, as the doorman will always sign for you and keep the package safe as if it were his own. Anything coming in and out is documented, making the margin of error very small. Many doormen will venture outside of the lobby to open taxi doors and carry in any bags that the tenants have in hand. Basically, anything to make life more comfortable regarding what comes in and out of the building for tenants, including the tenants themselves, is what the doorman is there for. That is, if the doorman is good at his job and is friendly and amicable to tenants, guests, and delivery folk.

As with any service job you need the right personality to deal with people and their quirks. In Manhattan the doorman can be part-time delivery man, part-time post office clerk, part-time private detective, and part-time psychiatrist. They tend to know exactly what is going on in every household. They observe arguments in the lobby between husband and wife. They witness the way in which each child is parented by the interaction between the parents and their offspring. They know exactly how kinky each household is by the oversized objects that don't fit into the mailbox but still need to be signed for with revealing packaging on the outside. They also know who goes in and out of each apartment, including drug dealers, high-class prostitutes, and rent boys.

The stories doormen are told each and every day in Manhattan buildings as excuses for wayward behavior by tenants are exceptionally unoriginal and obvious. "Doug, I am expecting a new cleaning lady called Trixie today at 11:00 p.m. Please—just let her up. You don't need to call, and it's a surprise for my wife so there is no need to mention it to her. Thanks."

"Does Trixie have a last name please, as I need to write it down in the book?" Complete silence. "Doug, I will give you something later, and I owe you one."

Doormen are also excellent private detectives when tenants want to spy on others in their household, and it's a lot cheaper to use the doorman instead of hiring a private eye. "Doug, please tell me if my husband comes back home after 10:00 p.m. when I am staying with my mother upstate and if he gets any suspicious packages?" Doug is of course not paid to do undercover detective work or to reveal bad behavioral habits of one tenant in regard to another. This type of extracurricular work would be frowned upon by the management company. The doormen usually ignore such requests, but in some cases will subtly reveal information that could be damaging without leaving any trace. There are potentially no secrets in a doorman building.

The therapist element usually involves those in therapy who can't get enough help simply because there are not enough hours in the day. They will ask the doorman the most ridiculous questions like, "Do you think I am pretty?" "Did you notice anything off about my girlfriend last night when she left?" "Am I fat?" "Should I buy my boyfriend this watch in the catalogue for his birthday or is that too much money?" Doormen do their best to answer the questions and become experts in answering knowing full well the reaction of the tenant. Therapists get paid fortunes for doing the work of a doorman, and the therapists normally only have to see their clients once or twice a week as opposed to the doorman who has to see the tenant in need at least five days a week and many times each day.

In a standard Manhattan doorman building, whether a rental, co-op, condo, or hybrid, there will be in place twenty-four-hour doorman coverage. Very high-end buildings have more than one doorman at any one time or will have a combination of one doorman and one porter or one doorman and one concierge. Really, it means there are two doormen on at the same time but one is called something else because of seniority or pay structure or actual job description. The doorman will only do doorman tasks but the porter and concierge may have other job responsibilities too as well as pretending to be doormen when asked.

In each twenty-four-hour period there are normally three shifts: The first one starts at 7:00 a.m. and ends at 3:00 p.m. and so witnesses the leaving for work and leaving for school, and hands tenants the morning newspapers. The middle shift is from 3:00 p.m. to 11:00 p.m. and is the busiest. It is the delivery-frenzy period, including dry cleaning, oversized mail from the USPS, UPS, and FedEx as well as the dinner-delivery stampede that occurs every night. The final shift is the graveyard shift from 11:00 p.m. to 7:00 a.m. This is also sometimes referred to as the "try not to fall asleep at the desk" shift as well as the "rescue drunken tenants from illicit activity" shift. Most senior doormen choose the first shift since it is a fine balance between normal working hours with an early going-home time and just enough work to keep them awake. Each doorman usually works five days a week with some having off weekends and some having their weekends during the week. Coverage for illness, vacation days, and lunch breaks comes from the other members of the staff in the building, of which there are many.

CHAPTER 4

Superintendents

Don't become enemies with the superintendent of your building (otherwise known as "The Super"). He is the oligarch of the building, in charge of anything and everything that moves. In small, nondoorman buildings, the super does everything from painting the hallways to taking out the trash and cleaning the stoop. If there is not enough work for him in a single building, he often has several that he looks after and keeps in working order. He will also do minor repairs to the building as well as to apartments. The elderly use the super a lot for changing light bulbs and fixing blocked sinks and toilets.

As with doormen, supers are mostly unionized, belonging to the all-powerful SEIU Local 32BJ, and are very difficult to terminate. The unions in the city are very effective in representing and protecting their members, and unless supers have stolen from the building or molested one of the tenants and you can prove it, they remain in their jobs for the whole of their working lives.

The benefits for a super go far and beyond that which is on offer for most employees in Manhattan. In the majority of cases, a super lives in the building as it is mandated by the city: "Any building over twelve units that has an owner who does not reside in the building must have a super on the property 24/7 or a super that lives no more than two hundred feet away."[1]

Supers used to be housed in the basement in substandard apartments, but with proper union representation and stricter housing regulations, the super's accommodations have improved dramatically in recent years. They live rent free as part of the perks of the job, and enjoy all the amenities of the building (fitness room, pool, laundry facilities) if they exist, for themselves and their families. They tend to hang on to their jobs for as long as university professors with tenure.

It is extremely useful having a super who lives in the building, because if anything goes wrong he can deal with it instantly since he is permanently on call—even if he is not on the premises. I recently found this out to be true in my own building. My youngest son thought it would be really funny to lock everyone out of the apartment as they were chasing our toddler down the communal hallway. A tasty chicken soup was left boiling on the stove. Of course, no one had a spare set of keys, and that included the fake ones left at the front desk (my wife, Janet, trusts no one). I was downstairs at the time, signing a credit card slip for delivery of some dinner for

---

[1]Dick Koral, secretary/treasurer for the New York City Superintendents Technical Association.

my wife and me, and was met by my whole family who had descended to the lobby to inquire if I was carrying keys. I answered with a question: "Why would I have keys on me when everyone else is at home?" Answering a question with a question annoys my wife at the best of times, and did so even more with the thought of the entire building burning down because of that unattended soup boiling away merrily on the stove. My wife huffed and puffed a little, and then took everyone upstairs in the elevator. As the doors closed she called out: "Get a locksmith. We'll be in the hallway."

The doorman was extremely helpful at this juncture, giving what he assured was the name of a reputable and quick-to-respond locksmith in Manhattan with whom the building had had dealings in the past. I used the telephone in the lobby to speak with the locksmith, who told me that he would be at the apartment within thirty minutes. I told him to call me if there was a problem at the front desk. I then went upstairs, throwing my youngest son a nasty glare, and told my wife that our temporary homeless situation would be rectified shortly. They were encamped in the hallway eating the dinner that had been delivered.

Returning to the lobby, I struck up a conversation with the doorman and thanked him for the locksmith referral. Forty-five minutes passed, and I called the locksmith again and this time asked him when exactly he would be arriving and how much his services would cost. He told me he would be arriving shortly, and that the cost would most likely not exceed $300. I asked him if shortly was really shortly or something more than shortly. My frustration, mixed in with a little skepticism and a small helping of sarcasm, wasn't met with any friendly retort. The forty-five-minute wait turned into an hour and then an hour and a quarter, accompanied by frequent visits by my nine-year-old daughter, who asked what the prognosis was, so as to report back to Mom upstairs.

My frustration began to turn to anger and despair, and the doorman with whom I had now become good friends noticed my gradual change in temperament. I casually asked him if anyone else had been locked out during his brief tenure in our building. He politely and informatively responded that three tenants had experienced similar problems. I then further asked if they had experienced similar delays in getting a locksmith over and whether it was the same locksmith. He looked at me and nonchalantly replied that they hadn't used a locksmith at all, and that the super had let them back in to their apartments. "With a key?" I asked. "No, with some special implement that he keeps here in the drawer for tenants when they get locked out," he chirped back. "Is the super at home?" I asked the doorman, raising my voice with a question-ending crescendo that shook the foundations of the building and frightened the doorman a little.

The super was indeed home, and came out thirty seconds after I called him. I was thinking about having a conversation with the doorman about why he didn't tell me about the super's tool in the first place, but instead I just looked at him and shook my head and shrugged my shoulders. The super opened the drawer of the doorman's desk, took out a strange-looking corrugated cardboard instrument, and headed for the elevator. I hastily called the locksmith and told him not to bother coming because the building had burned down due to the overcooked soup.

The super and I arrived at my floor and walked to our front door, stepping over the squatters who were still feasting on the take-out food and playing with the baby. Within five seconds, he had gained entry to our apartment without breaking the lock. I wondered: Did he work for 007? Was he a part-time magician? Was he the most successful burglar New York City had ever known? We would never know.

I slipped him a fifty and thanked him profusely as I ran into the kitchen and turned down the chicken soup that was cooking away at a hearty pace. When I turned around to thank the super again he had mysteriously disappeared. As supers do. He was on his way back home to his family or was solving the next crisis in the building. I was thinking he should wear a mask and a cape and be called "The Super Super."

This is one of the reasons why I stated at the beginning of this chapter not to become enemies with the super, as he can be in and out of your apartment in a matter of seconds and disappear with all your worldly possessions before you can say, "Holy super."

The super is in charge of the day-to-day running of the building, and is usually the highest paid employee there too. All doormen, porters, and maintenance crews report to him. He fills in when workers don't show up, and he normally has a tremendous amount of influence over the management company and the board. His pay is somewhat augmented because you tip him for everything he does.

Many supers work ridiculously long hours, and being on call 24/7 can't be fun. They rival doctors, investment bankers, and presidents for their commitment to the job. Manhattan residents can leave notes for the super at the front desk and go on their merry way knowing that somehow, magically, everything will get fixed in their absence. Supers are one of the many joys of living in Manhattan.

CHAPTER 5

Tipping for the Holidays

Service in Manhattan is usually excellent. It is the service capital of the world. So much stuff is delivered to all of our homes that we take the efficiency of the Manhattan marketplace for granted. Food, laundry, dry cleaning, meals, gifts, and even prescriptions from pharmacies are delivered day in and day out. Tipping, of course, takes place on a daily basis: when we order in food, ride in a taxi, visit a beauty salon, or eat out at a restaurant, the Manhattan consumer is faced with the decision of whether to and what to tip on a case-by-case basis.

Year-end tipping is somewhat different, as it should reflect services performed over a much longer time period and more frequently, and makes daily or weekly tipping redundant. What is apparent to each and every New Yorker is that in November the level of service from yearly tipped staff goes into a new stratosphere. Doors are opened much quicker, doormen are super friendly, staff go out of their way to help you, and you are treated like royalty on a daily basis. Around the beginning of December, chatter starts up among the tenants of the building you live in regarding tipping policy for workmen. This is also true for babysitters, parking attendants, and any other salesmen or deliverymen you use throughout the year. You start receiving holiday cards from staff in your building that list everyone who works there. The parking attendant stops you one evening to thrust a card into your hand, wishes you a happy Christmas, and tells you his name ten times in rapid succession.

Year-end tipping is a huge dilemma for many people, as it involves forking out large sums of money each year. It takes multiple trips to an ATM machine to withdraw enough funds to cover all the tips needed for distribution. After tips have been handed out, the level of service goes back to the same standard it was before, regardless of how well you have personally tipped the workers. (That is, unless, you haven't tipped them at all, either out of forgetfulness, or because you don't believe in the tipping system, or because you just didn't think an individual was worthy of a tip. No tip can lead to a confrontation further down the line, a decline in services going forward, and sometimes in extreme cases, a damaged car or mail going missing. It's always best to tip something reasonable to avoid strife.)

In large buildings the list of staff names can reach beyond a staggering fifty names. When looking over the list, don't be surprised to know very few of them. Some of them will be behind-the-scenes employees who work for the management company, those who man service entrances, and those who work during the wee hours of the night. There is no right or wrong amount to tip. As discussed, some people don't tip at all, but these Scrooges are well known by staff and are unlikely to receive the same kind of service as those who tip well. The golden rule is always tip the super and the doormen more than the porters and the other ancillary workers. The building staff do talk among one another and take their tips very seriously; it can make up a sizeable chunk of their yearly compensation, and tenants are on the whole appreciative of the work their building staff do for them during the year.

I used to live in a building that had 440 rental apartments, a huge, sprawling doorman-staffed building that covered an entire block on the Upper East Side. I owned a car that I kept in a parking garage around the corner, and I had a babysitter and a cleaning lady. The total number of people I needed to tip before the holidays was thirty-five in my building, eight in the parking garage, plus the two women who worked in my apartment. The bigger tips went to the super, the four doormen, the manager of the parking garage, and the babysitter and cleaning lady. In all, I spent over $2,000 in tips.

The consequences of the holiday tipping season were that my writing hand hurt from writing holiday cards, my tongue was dry from sealing too many envelopes, my spelling of Eastern European names had improved dramatically, and I had very little money left over to spend on my own family.

I calculated that a porter received about $20 on

average from every apartment in the building. He carries shopping, takes out the garbage, and does recycling, and can earn as much as $10,000 from tips at holiday time. New York City porters are most likely the highest paid porters in any city I know of when tips are included in the total compensation. Of course there are buildings that are much smaller and have fewer staff and so the cost of tipping is not so great for the tenants and the rewards for the staff are much lower.

Rental buildings are normally larger in size, so tenants need to build the cost of holiday tipping into their yearly expenditures when looking for an apartment and trying to economize and set budgets. Asking the landlord how many staff the building employs is a good place to start, and ask a neighbor in early December how much people in the building normally tip. Get a second opinion from friends or work colleagues who also live in the city and live in comparable buildings. Many tenants get very upset when they later find out that they overtipped because of a lack of partaking in the due diligence process. It's always good to be Joe Average in tipping and stay off any radar screen.

CHAPTER 6

Neighborhood Pride

A map of Manhattan contains numerous neighborhoods. The most basic divisions are between uptown, midtown, and downtown. Then there is the East
Side and West Side going horizontally across the city
with Fifth Avenue being the vertical dividing line. Within these basic partitions there are smaller but distinctive
neighborhoods: the West Village, Soho, Harlem, Spanish Harlem, the Upper West Side, Tribeca, Little Italy,
Chinatown, and Battery Park are just a few of them.

Rivalries really do exist. I live on the Upper East Side
of Manhattan and I can't tell you the number of times I
have been told by residents of the Upper West Side that
they could never live across town. When pressed for a
reason, I have heard explanations such as snobbery, too
much concrete, very cold people, lack of character, and
no vibe. I get very upset by these comments, as I find
none to be true. I have lived uptown on both sides of the
park, so I am an impartial judge. While all the allegations
against the Upper East Side are fabrications of the truth,

this is not the case in describing the Upper West Side as being crunchy, hippy, devoid of good restaurants, and way too spread out. The truth of the matter is these two uptown neighborhoods do have a different feel to them. Even though the various allegations made against other neighborhoods are exaggerated, there is an element of truth to them.

To distinguish between the various sectors of Manhattan, there has to be more than just geography to describe their differences. No two neighborhoods in Manhattan are the same, and it is the uniqueness of each little area that helps make this city so special.

Downtown folk are even more loyal and somewhat defensive about their neighborhoods. They claim to have to take their passports with them when they come uptown on either side of the park, and make jokes about having nosebleeds when they venture so far north. One of my friends who lives down in Tribeca tells me every time he comes up to my apartment that he doesn't understand why I would want to live on the Upper East Side, and that I might as well live in Connecticut. His theory is based on the fact that downtown has a much more vibrant nightlife and a much better selection of restaurants. He is right. I do argue with him that the flip side of losing out on a higher quality of entertainment at your doorstep is that raising kids is easier uptown than downtown. He won't even concede this point, arguing that this may be the case if you want to raise boring, uninspiring children.

Many Manhattan residents choose where they live in relation to proximity to subway stations and bus routes. Commuting within the city is made easier if there is a direct subway route from home to work. Others choose their location based on where their children will be schooled, because public school admittance is based on which zone you are situated in. For those with kids in private school, parents' nearness to schools is not as important, as many privately educated children are bused in from all over the city.

From an investment perspective, the old adage of "location, location, location" being the three most important criteria in looking for a home clearly comes into play—both where residents choose to live and how much they have to spend on housing. It is rare to find someone who lives in New York City who loves the city and hates the neighborhood he resides in. You get to know your neighborhood like the back of your hand and notice every subtle change that takes place. There is a tendency to do grocery shopping in the vicinity of where you live and to eat out at neighborhood restaurants.

When in the suburbs, however, most activities outside of the house involve getting in a car and driving to malls, supermarkets, and restaurants. When you live in New York City there are few valet-parking restaurants and no parking lots for supermarkets or department stores. Everyone walks. The sidewalks are brimming with pedestrians. Some suburban towns don't even have sidewalks. What's the point as everyone drives? Some of my work colleagues tell me nightmarish stories about late at night in the suburbs of running out of milk and having to get dressed, take the car out, drive a couple of miles to a supermarket, and get home thirty minutes later. When we run out of milk in Manhattan, I can choose which one of fifteen stores within three blocks that I can walk to and be back on the couch in ten minutes. If I am really lazy I can get the milk delivered and never have to leave my apartment. The reason why you become so attached to your neighborhood is because of all the conveniences surrounding you.

I have made a list of everything I do within walking distance to my apartment building. I am not insinuating that the Upper East Side is unique in the services that it offers its residents, as this is replicated in almost each and every neighborhood in Manhattan, but I don't know those areas as well. I mail my letters in the mailbox at the end of my street and buy stamps at the post office three blocks away. If I need an alternative method of shipping, all the major companies do pickups from my doorman downstairs. I buy my coffee at three different vendors all within a block of me. The bagel store is a stone's throw away. I like this particular bagel store rather than the other three within two blocks away. There is a convenience store in the middle of my block for candy, soda, newspapers, and the like. There are three pharmacies for prescriptions and any other health products at the end of the block. The vet's office for the cat is but two doors away. The pediatrician is located one block north and our general practitioner for us adults is two blocks farther up the road. My wife walks to the gym and passes two others on her way there, and buys the meat from the butcher on the way home. I can shop at five supermarkets within a three-minute walk and purchase wine at the four liquor stores nearby. I get my haircut on my block and my wife and daughters use the nail salon one block away. The buses heading downtown or uptown or crosstown are all less than two blocks away. The subway is three blocks away.

I have just returned from walking three blocks in either direction from my house and counted seventy-two restaurants that I can eat at and leave and be home five minutes later. That doesn't include the sixteen bars that also serve food. There are five movie theatres that I can walk to, one comedy club, and two nightclubs. The dry cleaner picks up and delivers, but if he didn't I could choose between seven that are within three blocks of me. I walk to the ice cream store with the kids as well as to the specialty cheese store and the pet store to buy the cat some treats. The only thing not in walking distance that I use on a weekly basis is the gas station, which is fifteen blocks away, but then why would I walk there?

So everything is at our fingertips. Life can't get any easier for able-bodied NYC residents. New York City is without doubt the convenience city of the world. You would think that with this type of lifestyle, its population would be lazy, idle, and obese. The latest figures from New York State Behavioral Risk Factor Surveillance System show that Manhattan has the lowest percentage of overweight residents of any of the sixty-two New York State counties. Even though all of our daily needs can be met just around the corner, we still have to walk and exercise to make use of it.

Living on Eightieth Street, I rarely venture north of Eighty-sixth Street and rarely south of Seventy-second Street. Anything outside of a seven-to-ten block radius,

I consider to be a different neighborhood than the one I live in. I hardly know a single restaurant or where a pharmacy is located in the sixties or nineties on the East Side. When I lived on Eighty-fifth Street, most of my activities took place south of Eighty-sixth Street and north of Seventy-ninth. This doesn't mean that I won't venture out, as I love to go downtown and see what is new, and we cross over to the West Side and see friends all the time. When I moved from Eighty-fifth Street to Eightieth Street five years ago, I thought I had moved towns. I had to find a new dry cleaner, new neighborhood restaurants, and a new supermarket to visit. I had only moved five small blocks away on the same avenue yet everything seemed foreign to me. I rarely go back to the diners, restaurants, and bars that knew me by name and order, and when I move again the same thing will happen. This is a phenomenon unique to New York City as residents define their neighborhoods within a very small area.

Many of the more traditional neighborhoods such as German Town, Little Hungary, and Little Italy, as well as the Jewish presence on the Lower East Side, have receded quite dramatically. Chinatown has all but swallowed up one street of Little Italy, and one restaurant and one butcher remain as a reminder of a huge German population between Seventy-ninth and Eighty-sixth streets on the East Side. New immigrants settled there after the war and raised their children, who then became more prosperous and moved out of the city when it was in decline in the '70s. They never came back. Without loyal customers who wish to shop for goods they used to buy in the old country, the neighborhoods decline. First the older generations die off and are replaced by a different wave of immigrants. Then the stores that supported these folk shutter their doors for good and are replaced by the needs of new and different residents. All that is left is a memory of once was.

PART 2

Transportation

CHAPTER 7

New York Has a Monorail?

Arriving in New York City by air is not at all glamorous. The three airports that service this great city are run down, decrepit, and mundane places to spend time before or after a flight. For such a great metropolitan urban sprawl, it is pretty shocking to note that apart from a rickety old bus, there is not a single other direct route into Manhattan via any other means of public transportation. In most other cities around the world, you have monorails, high-speed trains, boats, luxury buses, and subway systems that transport millions of people right into the heart of the city center from the outlying airports. The best New York can offer is a recently built monorail that picks you up via another monorail and takes you right into the heart of Jamaica. Not the Jamaica that is the reggae capital of the world with great beaches, but the area of Queens that no one ever visited before because there is nothing there.

Once in Jamaica, one is left to fend for oneself in an urgent quest to locate the New York subway system for an hour's ride into the city, stopping at so many stations that you actually lose count.

I once flew from Boston to New York's JFK airport by an express plane that took one hour and ten minutes gate to gate. I then walked for twenty minutes inside the terminal building trying to follow the signs to the monorail, but got lost twice and ended up back at luggage retrieval one time and in the taxi line on the other attempt. After being personally escorted by an airport worker to the entrance to the monorail, I was on my way.

I waited ten minutes for the tubular-like contraption to arrive. I embarked and decided to stand for the duration. There were two other passengers and in true traveling style, we all headed for different corners of the compartment to avoid any possibility of eye contact or, God forbid, conversation. The doors closed after a five-minute wait, and the fifteen-minute journey to Jamaica began. We were elevated above such fascinating New York sights as the JFK Expressway and the Van Wyck Expressway. The monorail did not zoom to its destination. I think it is purposely run slow because in testing this prototype it fell off the rail and killed one of the drivers. It is now set at a pace slightly quicker than walking, but definitely slower than a medium-speed bike.

The monorail came to a stop and a muffled voice made an announcement saying this was the end of the line. I expected to at least see the Manhattan skyline, but instead all I saw were run-down stores, smoke rising from some tenement buildings, and lots of people asking if you wanted a taxi. I thought to myself: "I am sure I could have taken a taxi from JFK. So why would I want to take a taxi from here?" I looked for signs to the subway, and eventually found them at the end of the platform. I went down some stairs, up some stairs, and down some more stairs. It reminded me of my arrival at JFK where I had followed the same routine on getting off the plane. I was beginning to think that in Queens the only way of getting anywhere was to go down-up-down. So my mind wandered off to why this was so. I had seen many mothers and strollers at JFK who could not use the stairs or escalators but needed the elevator instead. They spent the next twenty minutes going down-up-down, instead of my five minutes, as they had to wait for elevators, walk, and then wait again.

I eventually found the entrance to the subway station and bought a ticket. I waited on the platform for the subway train to arrive. Twelve minutes later, it arrived and I sat down in a sparsely populated car for the continuation of my arduous journey to midtown Manhattan. I looked at a map and located Jamaica because of its close proximity to a plane-like object. Then I realized that I had found LaGuardia. Boy, were they close together on the map. They were only seven fingers apart from each other, and yes, I did measure it. I then tried to count how many stops until Times Square. I was doing OK until I actually lost the train line somewhere after Roosevelt Island and had to go back and start again. It was a lot anyway. And it was frightfully boring.

There was nothing to look at and no interesting advertisements at all. In fact, most of them were in Spanish advertising schools to learn English. The problem with this advertisement was that no one who spoke English could understand the advert. I asked a fellow passenger what the ad was for and he responded in pidgin English that he didn't speak English. But he did say "Inglese" five times while pointing at the advert, so from that I gathered it was an advert for a school teaching English. He then promptly got up from his seat and sat at the other end of the compartment. I had obviously broken the subway code of silence. I then did something far worse. I smiled at him when the train reached the next stop. He got up from his seat, left the compartment, and I saw that he quickly ran into the next one before the doors closed. I am happy for him that he narrowly missed having to re-engage in any form of communication with the crazy guy with the suitcase.

One hour and ten minutes later the subway train arrived at Times Square, but by that point I was so disorientated, and half-asleep, that I didn't understand the announcement. I just heard a garbled voice saying, "This is Forty-second Street. Change here for the 1, 2, 3, 9, 15, A, B, C, D, E, U, V, W, and S trains." Why was the S out of sequence? I wondered. And then it hit me: I was at my destination. But the doors had shut and the train moved off. A man's voice then came over the loudspeaker saying, "This train is now express. Next stop is … ," and then I couldn't make out what he said, but I believe it was "somewhere you don't want to be."

I got off somewhere in the Village, and with my heavy suitcase being pulled behind me, I climbed thirty-six steps to the surface and promptly hailed a taxi to take me home. It had taken me almost two hours to get there, which was fifty minutes longer than the flight. I had spent almost as much money on public transportation, including the taxi, as I would have done on the flat fare from JFK to the city.

I would never be taking that mode of transportation again.

CHAPTER 8

Taxi!

From the Airport

After decades of complaints, New York City's authorities finally realized that some unscrupulous taxi drivers had a tendency to stray from the most direct route from JFK airport to the city. As a consequence, many unsuspecting tourists were taken on the more "scenic" route to town, resulting in hundred-dollar taxi rides. Taxi drivers had been known to pile three or four customers into their cabs at the airport, and charge them $50 each for dropping them off at various different points in the city. Tourists were getting ripped off, and the New York City Taxi and Limousine Commission (TLC) decided in one fell swoop to rid these corrupt practices.

So in the earliest part of this century, a fixed rate from JFK to Manhattan was introduced as mandatory to all taxis operating under license in the city.

The commission obviously thought really long and hard about this. All the ardent criminals in the taxi business naturally operated on the same route. Every other journey was relatively free of corruption. Not nearly as many complaints came from the LaGuardia or Newark routes into the city, and within Manhattan taxi drivers always went the most direct route without question. The logic was that if you regulated JFK to Manhattan, then everything else would fall into place. Drivers would be warier about taking their customers for "a ride."

I can honestly say that this regulation has definitely sped up the journey by taxi to Manhattan from JFK. Taxi drivers now know exactly what they can earn, and so they try to complete the journey in the quickest amount of time. Unfortunately, the result is they drive so recklessly on this route, and use their horn at least eight times a second, that when you arrive at your destination your hair is standing on end, and you hear beeping ringing around your head for days after. So while this flat rate may be cheaper and more regulated, it is certainly much more hazardous to your health. I have been in taxis from JFK that have traveled most of the expressway and parkway on the hard shoulders. I have traveled trailing an ambulance for five miles and have been in a taxi whose driver did not once take his hand off the horn for the whole duration of the journey.

In the City

The busiest times of the day for taxis are between 7:30 a.m. and 9:30 a.m., and then again between 4:00 p.m.

and 7:00 p.m., Monday to Friday. This is quite easily explained by rush-hour activity by the New York commuter. Many who live in Manhattan use the resourcefulness of the New York taxi to take them from their homes to their places of work. It is of course the most convenient form of transport: getting picked up in close proximity to your place of abode, and depositing you somewhat close to your chosen destination.

There are other times when you see a whole stream of vacant taxicabs driving aimlessly up or down avenues, jockeying for nonexistent passengers. Monday nights after 9:00 p.m. are a prime example. Most folk are relaxing at home on a Monday night after the arduous first day after the weekend, many watching football during the fall and winter. Armies of empty cabs with bright yellow "vacant" beacons prominently displayed on top are scanning the horizon looking for anyone leaving a restaurant or bar. They lie in wait like a wild cat surveying a possible kill, and then pounce on their victim with cheetah-like speed.

Contrast this with the mad scramble during rush hour, when it is the people on the streets who fight over vacant cabs. It is amazing how common folk change their behavior when they presume that wrongdoing is about to or has just happened to them. I have on many occasions seen ordinary folk in suits and dresses screaming and cursing at each other in the street arguing about who saw the vacant cab first. The driver, impatient at the bickering, sees another customer half a block up the street with his right hand extended, and decides he can't be bothered to wait until the two arguers have finished insulting one another. He promptly drives off and picks up one lucky customer who has benefited from others' lack of common sense and decency. (Not once do the other two ask each other where they are going, and the question of sharing a cab doesn't even enter their minds.)

There is something about empty cabs during rush hour that presents a challenge to native New Yorkers and makes their pupils pop out of their eyes in their pursuit of victory. You can see armies of customers lined up on Park Avenue jostling for position, walking farther and farther away from their destinations in order to outsmart their opponents. When one dim yellow "vacant" light is spotted in the distance, a steady trot is replaced by the unattractive sight of a stampede of human traffic. Just as the hoards of desperate potential passengers arrive at the empty cab, the driver, fearing for his life, puts on the "occupied" sign and speeds off, leaving the despairing masses cursing the previously free taxi that has moved on.

The problem with New York taxis is not that there is a shortage of cabs. Just look outside the Waldorf-Astoria Hotel and see the blocks of cabs lined up waiting for passengers to emerge from their hotel rooms to do business in areas of the city not in walking distance. The real issue is that there are two shifts in New York, and there is no equitable time to change shifts without upsetting one or two of the drivers. A New York taxi is usually on the roads of the city for twenty-four hours a day, seven days a week. There are two twelve-hour shifts shared equally between two drivers. The shift changes occur at 5:00–6:00 a.m. and 5:00–6:00 p.m. That allows one driver to engage in the morning rush hour and one in the afternoon one. The problem is, the driver ending the early shift has to reach the chosen destination of the second driver between the hours of 4:30 p.m. and 5:30 p.m., thus displaying a "busy" light atop their cabs. I am convinced the TLC has fervently debated this issue and has yet to come up with an answer that satisfies both the drivers and the passengers. As a result, there is nothing more frustrating than watching hoards of empty taxis drive by during peak hours in order to get to the next driver who wants to begin his shift.

There are locations where your chances of getting a cab increase dramatically. Many of the taxi drivers live in Queens, and the taxi companies that own them operate out of Long Island City, just across the Fifty-ninth Street Bridge. The shift change often takes place in Queens at the taxi depot. So just after the changeover has taken place, the new shift driver quickly gets into his cab and crosses the bridge into Manhattan to find his first customer of the day. On entering Manhattan, he immediately confronts traffic on Second Avenue and so proceeds to head west on one of the cross streets in the sixties. Hence you find a plethora of vacant cabs in the sixties at 5:30 p.m. each weekday around Lexington and Park avenues. Those in the know walk up from their office blocks in the fifties to these intersections and walk eastward to catch the free taxis. The change of shifts also takes place at major subway stations, particularly on the Upper East Side of Manhattan at the Eighty-sixth Street subway station. This is because the second shift driver arrives by subway and the first shift driver needs the subway to return home.

A little warning to potential customers about the hazards of hailing a cab during shift changes: Do not ever try to approach first-shift drivers sitting in their cabs awaiting the driver for the second shift. The first-shift driver is extremely irritable for many a reason: Perhaps he has not made enough money in his shift. Or the second-shift driver is late. Maybe the second-shift driver left the first-shift driver an empty gas tank twelve hours previous. The first-shift driver might have received a ticket from a traffic warden. The first-shift driver could be late for his second job. There exists a host of scenarios as to why you should not approach first-shift drivers at the end of their shifts.

The question is, how do you tell the difference between a first-shift driver and a second-shift one? The answer is quite simple: A first-shift driver, although irritated, isn't trying to get ready for his shift. He will not be adjusting his seat, nor the rearview mirror, nor attaching an EZPass to his windshield (although he may be detaching an EZPass, which can be quite confusing). The key is to be patient and wait until the second-shift driver looks ready to turn his light on, and try to establish eye contact with him momentarily before the process begins.

One also has to be on the lookout for potential taxi-ride thieves lurking within half a block of your chosen taxi. As soon as the light comes on, if you see anyone charging toward the taxi door with flapping arms screaming out the word "taxi!" then you have been besmirched by the inevitable taxi grab. In a flash, the door will open and close and the taxi will speed off, with you left standing on the sidewalk wondering how on earth that could have happened.

New York taxi drivers have a reputation for being dreadful drivers, weaving in and out of traffic and getting into far too many accidents and causing their own passengers heart attacks, as well as frightening the life out of fellow drivers, cyclists, and pedestrians. It is hard enough driving in New York City as a recreational driver [see Chapter 10]. Just imagine if you had to do it for a living seven days a week for twelve hours a day. So I understand why a taxi driver can be hotheaded behind the wheel. There is also a misconception that time is money. The cab driver has convinced himself and others that the faster he gets from point A to point B, the more money he will earn. The starting fare of $2.50 certainly adds weight to this argument. But the recent introduction of being paid for waiting time on the meter while being stuck in traffic helps to negate it. As long as the taxi has a passenger, then the driver is earning money, and some of the erratic driving can be connected to a quest to find passengers when empty.

The makeup and ethnicity of New York City cab drivers follows very closely the latest wave of immigration to the city. The previous statement does not imply that all taxi drivers are immigrants, but in New York a large percentage of the drivers are recent immigrants. The waves of immigration into New York have been reflected by Russian drivers in the '70s, Israeli drivers in the '80s, and Asian drivers in the '90s, closely followed by West African and Haitian drivers in the beginning of the twenty-first century. Remnants of each wave remain, and you generally never hear the same language twice when entering more than one cab in the same day.

The immigrant status of taxi drivers is relevant to the driving behavior of taxi drivers. I am not asserting that immigrants are bad drivers. Far from it, considering I, an immigrant from London, England who moved to New York City in 1995, am an excellent driver!

However, the vast majority of new taxi drivers have never driven a car in their country of origin. They mostly come from poorer countries where the percentage of the population owning a car is small, and the possibility of renting one is virtually nonexistent. They apply for a job as a taxi driver in New York because there is very little need for command of the English language and few qualifications are required. They take a New York State driving test in a short amount of time and are on the roads with a limited total of driving-time experience. We then entrust ourselves to their driving skills day in and day out, not knowing how long they have spent behind the wheel.

The biggest question I have for all taxi drivers is: Who on earth are you talking to on your cell phones? The first time I got into a New York City taxi I honestly thought the driver was talking to me in a strange language that I couldn't understand. I asked him what language he was speaking and he replied it was Arabic. For the entire duration of the journey I kept saying to him, "Sorry, are you talking to me?" and "I really don't understand what you are saying." The fact is, taxi drivers spend all day on the cell phone. Are they talking to their wives? Are they talking to friends? Or, as I now believe, are they talking to other taxi drivers, which would explain why they are always on the phone. The city did ban the use of non-hands-free cell phones so that the taxi driver would keep both hands on the steering wheel at all times, and the consequence of this is that it now looks like every taxi driver is talking to himself when you see them sitting in the driver's seat merrily chatting away in a whole array of foreign languages.

The problem occurs when a conversation needs to be conducted between those who speak one language in the front and those who speak another in the back. The pronunciation of numbers can lead to costly mistakes.

"Where to, please?" asks the driver in heavily accented English.

"Eightieth Street, please," the passenger replies.

"Cross street?" the driver retorts.

"Third Avenue, please," the passenger responds, feeling confident of arriving on time for a very important meeting. He doses off and is awoken by the driver saying that they have arrived. The passenger looks around and starts freaking out. "Eightieth, not Eighteenth Street! Eightieth Street! One greater than Seventy-ninth. The Upper East Side, not the Village!"

The two of them then proceed to argue with voices rising to a crescendo, cursing and screaming at one another. The argument continues for as long as the journey originally took, and still the passenger is nowhere near his destination. Eventually they both agree to head up Third Avenue to where the passenger originally planned on being, and on arrival pay the driver three times as much as it would have cost if there hadn't been a breakdown in language. The passenger has to pay for the wrong journey, the waiting time for arguing, and the corrected journey to the proper final destination. Only in New York.

Believe it or not, the number of New York City taxis is set by law at 11,787, and not a single new taxi license has been issued in over half a century. The symbol of this most regulated of industries is the medallion, which is bolted to the hood of the taxi. This is the proof of the license. The cost of purchasing a medallion has now passed the average price of a one-bedroom apartment in Manhattan: a cool half a million dollars. In these economic times, what is interesting is that the value of a taxi medallion only seems to go up in value because of regulated and strict supply restrictions, as compared to a one-bedroom apartment that fluctuates with starting salaries at Wall Street firms. Such is the case of an asset whose supply is limited by legislation, ensuring that its value can really only go up. The only threat seems to be if the amount of licenses is suddenly increased. But if it hasn't happened in fifty years, the chance of it happening now seems remote.

The way in which the spoils of taxi ownership are passed down is similar to that of any class system, whereby the owners do very well, the middlemen take their cut, and the users who do most of the legwork go home with very little apart from a lot of blood, sweat and tears. The owners will charge the taxi companies a monthly fee for the right to use the license to drive a taxi in the city. The yield for the owners varies between 5 and 8 percent. The taxi companies then recruit drivers and charge them anywhere from $85 to $135 a session for the right to drive the taxi. The only thing that is fixed is what the driver can charge the passenger. That is set out on the information sheet stuck to the back of the divide in the taxi, and regulated by the TLC. This is trickle-down economics in full force. Everybody gains from passing the buck down the chain, with the wealthy buying the medallion earning a nice yield and an almost guaranteed increase in the value of the asset. The manager can then charge his drivers a market rate to generate enough profit for himself and generate enough demand for drivers, and the TLC set the rate enabling the whole formula to work. If only all other industries worked as well under the capitalist system.

The taxi system works very efficiently and effectively. It occasionally breaks down when the cost of fuel and insurance and maintenance of the cabs outpaces the amount charged via the meter. However, strikes are few and far between, and most disputes seem to be resolved well before they hit the headlines in the NYC newspapers, usually by a small increase in the standard fare with occasional extra charges to passengers thrown in.

CHAPTER 9

Car Services

The shepherding of passengers in cars in the city is not just restricted to yellow cabs. Car service companies with hoards of town cars operate with many restrictions in Manhattan. Large accounts used to exist between these car companies and the big Wall Street firms. During the good times, not only the Wall Street executives, but their wives, kids, mothers-in-law, and nannies benefited from these outlandish expense accounts. This came to a crashing halt when Wall Street firms began cutting expenses and putting an end to bad press. The car service companies suffered tremendously as nannies now had to take regular yellow cabs paid for out of the pockets of their employers rather than their employers' employers.

A car service has to be booked either on the phone or online, and then properly dispatched. A car service cannot legally drive up and down Park Avenue or any other New York City street looking for potential customers. The drivers of car services are not allowed to solicit business from the sidewalk. In this way, they do not compete with the yellow cabs. The laws are decided upon by the aforementioned TLC, and these laws are explained on its Web site for all to review. The problem is, you need a PhD in order to decipher them, and last I checked neither the owners, nor the dispatchers, nor the drivers are remotely qualified in knowing who can do what to whom and where. Even with all these restrictions and prohibitions against acting like cab drivers, every working day and at hot spots on weekends you find car services acting illegally, stealing rides from yellow cabs: thus the term "gypsy cab."

Since 1990, over 180 gypsy-cab drivers have been killed, almost two every year. They are usually licensed drivers working for one of the many legal car service companies in the city who are idle and go in search of work. They tend to go looking for work in areas that are lacking in yellow cabs and have reputations for being neighborhoods where you wouldn't want to pick up strays anyway. And so these drivers do occasionally pick up the wrong person. Not some deranged killer or a common thief looking for the day's takings, but an inspector from the TLC who will wave down the driver of a town car and slap him with a fine for attempting to break the bylaws. Yes. The Limo Police.

The one thing the car service companies do possess is really easy-to-remember phone numbers. They own many of the phone numbers with the same seven numbers, so if you lose 90 percent of your brain function and don't remember your name or address and are stranded with no money and just a cell phone on the streets of Manhattan, the likelihood is you may press the same number seven times in some delusional fashion and end up talking to an operator at a car service company. Of course, when asked your name, contact number, and where you want to be picked up, you can't remember.

Car services do provide a very useful service: getting you to the airport. They show up at doorsteps usually on time with a clean car and empty trunk. They are a dependable form of transport and should be guaranteed to show up, thus ensuring that flights are not missed because of transportation issues. Car services also provide invaluable transportation needs to those arriving at New York City airports. They provide a luxury service to valuable clients jetting in, the likes of which don't want to deal with the hassle of lines and language and fighting with other passengers waiting for yellow taxis. They also relieve an enormous amount of pressure on the taxi system as at times, particularly at the airports during bad weather, demand for transportation far outweighs supply.

Not all car service companies are the same. They differ in how they pick you up at the airport. There are those drivers that we have all seen proudly displaying the passenger's name on a board held closely to the driver's chest, which he then points in the direction of everyone emerging from baggage claim in an attempt to catch the passenger's eye. There are those who do the same, but stand strategically closer to where the plane has disembarked, before arriving at baggage control, so that they can help the passenger with their bags, combining driving and porter services. The problem with these two types of service is then you have to accompany the driver into the parking lot and pay for parking, sometimes walking for long periods and paying extra for parking because maybe the bags were delayed or the driver showed up early to get you.

Then there are those drivers/companies who refuse to stand at arrival terminals, and try to save the passenger money by not parking but instead arranging a place to meet the passenger. Those who have ordered a car service are requested to retrieve their bags and then call the easy-to-remember seven-digit number, recite the previously handed out confirmation number, and then listen to instructions regarding the number of the car and where he will be meeting you. It is a lot to remember and leaves enormous room for error. Many customers wander aimlessly outside terminal buildings looking for a specific black Lincoln Town Car, with twenty identical ones parked at the designated area.

Finally, there is the car whose driver won't even temporarily stop at the meeting place but just drives around the terminal building holding with a sign in the passenger window displaying your name, honking loudly to attract attention so as to find the right passenger to pick up.

All in all, car services are an excellent way to get to and from the airport. Ask your friends for a recommendation. Although you might be paying a little bit more, it saves the anxiety of finding a taxi on the way out to the airport, and guarantees that the drive home from the airport will not be spent driving at top speed behind an ambulance.

CHAPTER 10

Owning and Parking a Car in the City

Owning a car is a thrill—it gives you the freedom and ability to drive on the open road at any time, to wherever you may choose to go. But being able to spontaneously hop in your car and go is not the case in New York City. Owning a car in Manhattan is far from convenient, and is a prime example of the vast difference between living in the suburbs and living in the city.

For instance, a suburban family usually unlocks a door to their connecting garage, clicks a button to open the garage door, and embarks on a journey in no time. In Manhattan, with most parking garages you have to give at least an hour's advance warning to get your car out. This involves making a phone call and explaining to the parking attendant who answers the phone your account number, make of car, color of car, and the time you need the car. On many occasions, even after one hour's notice, you turn up to get your vehicle, strolling nonchalantly into the parking garage in anticipation of seeing your car ready to go, only to see a complete shambles in front of your eyes. Your phone call to order your car coincided with seven cars arriving for short-term parking, leaving the solitary attendant with no clue where to put these visiting machines and a huge backlog of cars needing to be delivered up front for anxiously awaiting monthly paying customers, including yourself.

Value for money doesn't always figure in car ownership in Manhattan. Many who own cars would shudder if they paused for a moment and calculated how much their car actually costs them per month and what it translates to in cost per usage. Making certain assumptions, I will say that the car being examined is a leased car and not owned and, using conservative numbers, nothing was put down at time of purchase. Let's say it costs $500 a month to lease, and that car insurance in Manhattan is approximately $150 a month. Let's assume that the car owner spends $100 per month on gas and $500 a month on garaging it overnight in the city at one of the numerous parking garages dotted around Manhattan. Servicing and oil changes and damage costs are waived as they are covered under the guarantee. Let's also assume that the driver uses tolls on his journeys at a cost of $75 a month and that at holiday times he has to tip the entire staff of the garage $600, translating into $50 a month. Adding in car washes and miscellaneous expenses of parking fines, speeding tickets, and other parking garage charges of a further $50 a month, this translates into just over $1,400 a month paid out for the privilege of car ownership.

The average Manhattan resident uses his car on weekends, taking it out on a Friday night or Saturday morning and returning it on Sunday. So let's assume he takes his car out five times during the month. That is a whopping $281 per use, which works out as far more expensive than renting a car each time one is needed. I am not advocating giving up car ownership in Manhattan as this is certainly a status symbol, and many do use their cars every day for reverse commutes to work outside of the city and to take their kids to and from school. But in this light, owning a car in Manhattan is indeed a luxury that the car owner has to pay through the nose to maintain.

The cheaper alternative to keeping a car in a parking garage is the free option—to find a spot for the car on the street. In this scenario, you must constantly move the car in accordance with the opposite-side-of-the-street parking regulations to avoid fines and having your car towed. Those who opt for alternate-side-of-the-street parking are a strange breed indeed. These people spend hours every week perusing the streets in search of a parking space, with knowledge of every fire hydrant and driveway and which side of the street is applicable to each day. They don't want to pay the $500 a month charges for garaging their car as they find this cost offensive and just simply unaffordable, yet they insist on keeping a car in the city. Their favorite line is: "If I lived in the suburbs I could park it in my driveway for free." So I say to this whole group of time wasters: "Leave!" In any other society a driver behind the wheel of a slow-moving vehicle going around neighborhood streets time after time, day after day would be prosecuted for curb crawling and loitering without intent.

Every night before a change in the cleaning-of-the-streets schedule, drivers are forced to leave the comfort of their apartments and move their cars. For many of these drivers the most successful event of the week is finding a free space on a Thursday night, which means that they don't have to move their car until the following Monday night.

Those who park on the street can spend their whole lives completely engrossed in the opposite-side-of-the-street schedule. They constantly monitor Web sites that announce suspensions in opposite-side-of-the-street parking regulations, and look forward to religious holidays when these rules are suspended for their duration.

I have been to a family's home who uses this bizarre parking system. I walked into their apartment and turned around to close the front door only to find a map of their neighborhood pinned to the back. In this case there was a cut-out car placed on the map showing the exact location of the car and a calendar next to it displaying when it had to be moved. It really was ingenious, practical, and very much a part of this family's life. It is something so unique to New York life that it is very difficult to explain to anyone who lives in the suburbs.

Parking for Visitors

There are many outside of the city who enjoy visits to Manhattan and like the flexibility of driving their own car across our bridges and tunnels. Then they look for parking, and are surprised at the lack of available free parking spaces, and simply don't carry enough quarters on them to park for one hour using a parking meter on the main avenues. They fail to realize that they are competing against a whole army of Manhattan residents who are already using the opposite-side-of-the-street system. The out-of-town drivers are then forced to use a parking garage that purposely charges a fortune for nonmonthly residents.

The out-of-towners leave their car and go out to eat or shop or go to the theatre, and return to their vehicles all happy after an evening's entertainment. They chat merrily with their spouses and friends, handing in their parking ticket for payment, and when the attendant interjects with the cost of the two-hour stay, a look of amazement quickly turning to anger appears on the face of the driver. This is immediately followed by screaming and shouting and refusals to pay such an exorbitant sum. The driver assumes that there has been a mistake and is then shown the charge list on the wall by the attendant, who is familiar with "out-of-town-driver parking charge shock."

The drivers pay the $50–$60, leaving the garage in a rage and swearing never to return to the city again so long as they live. But invariably, the delights of the city's many lures outweigh the remembrance of outrage, and the next time they come into the city they again drive in, but this time they refuse to leave their car in a parking garage, driving around in circles for two hours looking for a space, missing their show and dinner reservations.

In New York the motto for parking is "Pay up and shut up." And don't forget to tip the attendant, as he doesn't set the rates and depends on these tips to live.

CHAPTER 11

Driving and Traffic Tips

Driving a car in Manhattan is similar to driving an automobile in any other big city around the globe. The streets are overcrowded with far too many vehicles on the road. Drivers in Manhattan tend to be aggressive, and the quality of the roads is lower than outside of the city. Driving a car along the wide avenues, one frequently encounters trucks, buses, taxis, irate bike riders, and other struggling private-car drivers. On the narrow cross side streets of Manhattan one encounters all of the above with the exception of buses.

As long as one stays within the numbered streets of Manhattan, which means one tries not to venture too far north or south, then navigating one's way around is fairly simple, made easier by a grid system. With that being said, one frequently sees out-of-state drivers scratching their heads, displaying a somewhat confused demeanor, weaving across the avenues, and making turns into the side streets from the middle lane. Out-of-state license plates are scorned upon by local residents for their lack of aggression and their failure to understand the nuances of driving in the city. These nuances include but are not limited to:

- The timing of one's speed on avenues so as to make green lights and drive long stretches without stopping.
- Not letting anyone in and not being courteous to other drivers, even if one's own life depended on it.
- Harassing pedestrians crossing the street, even if the lights infer that the pedestrians have the right-of-way, especially when one needs to make a turn.
- Honking continuously if someone makes a driving mistake.
- Double-park every time one needs to drop something off or pick something up quickly, even if a free, legal space exists.
- Always weave in and out of traffic to find the fastest route without any regard for other drivers.
- Purposely make life difficult for taxi drivers and try to out-honk them.

Following these hard-and-fast rules won't necessarily achieve the aim of getting the driver from point A to point B without avoiding a major accident, but they will ensure that the driver will gain respect from other Manhattan drivers.

The condition of the roads in Manhattan is dreadful at best and is seasonally variable. Cracks from wear and tear appear after the summer, when the tarmac, concrete, and asphalt have been hard-baked by the sun and then stretched out as it cools into the fall. When snow arrives in winter, these cracks get filled by snow and ice, stretching the cracks even further. When the spring thaw hits Manhattan, the somewhat meaningless cracks have transformed themselves into giant potholes, capable of swallowing up small vehicles and medium-sized adults. Car drivers tend to see these potholes at the last moment, causing huge gyrations of vehicles seconds before they are about to disappear into the pothole underworld, or get smashed to pieces by the impact. With time, one gets to remember the most serious potholes so that one can position the vehicle in an alternate lane to avoid the giant swerve. However, this is a pretty futile exercise since other drivers who don't know the pothole locations have to react at the last minute to their impending doom and swerve into your automobile, causing a knock-on effect from all surrounding vehicles.

Some avenues are quicker than others, simply because they are wider and, in certain cases, less used. Sometimes using the avenues can be faster than taking the two express highways that flank both sides of Manhattan. On the east side there is the FDR and on the west side there is the Henry Hudson. For the most part, these two faster roads have no traffic lights, especially on the FDR, and were built to alleviate the buildup of traffic on the avenues that are supposed to be for more local use. The problem is that traffic can and does build up very quickly on these highways, so much so that cars are often stuck there for long periods of time. This phenomenon isn't exclusive to rush-hour periods either.

You can be driving down the FDR at 10:00 at night and encounter huge delays. More often than not these hold-ups aren't even mentioned on the many local traffic announcements on the radio, and what makes the process even more frustrating is that you can be sitting in a traffic jam for ages without explanation and then suddenly the road clears without ever knowing what caused the holdup in the first place.

Traffic builds up in the city in a heartbeat. The highways are the most prone to congestion, mostly because of the sheer volume of traffic, but there are some hidden escape routes and alternative options. Say traffic is backed up on the FDR all the way from 49th Street to 125th Street, and you need to zoom uptown to take the RFK Bridge (formerly known as the Triborough Bridge). Instead of sitting there for hours, try driving up Third Avenue and taking the left turn onto 124th Street to sneak on the RFK by the back door. Similarly, the Henry Hudson has a tendency of turning into one of the world's largest parking lots, with masses of stationary traffic patiently waiting to cross into New Jersey via the George Washington Bridge. Instead of wasting an entire early evening gazing at the adjacent Hudson River and seeing the bridge glistening tantalizingly on the horizon, try getting off the highway on the Upper West Side and taking either Riverside Drive or West End Avenue as slightly quicker alternatives.

These suggestions are not guaranteed to hasten one's journey and can end up taking even longer, but they do break the monotony for those who have to endure Manhattan traffic daily.

There is, of course, one time of the week when it is impossible to avoid traffic and that is on Friday afternoon, especially in the summer, when every car in Manhattan and others thrown in for annoyance are trying to leave the city. It really is reminiscent of a modern-day exodus that takes place every Friday from 4:00 p.m. to 8:00 p.m., week in and week out. It seems that at 4:00 p.m. everyone stops what he or she is doing and has a sudden urge to jump in a car and leave Manhattan for forty-eight hours before returning. Voices inside Manhattan residents' heads start repeating over and over again: "Get in your car. You must leave the city now." These drivers find themselves engulfed in a Friday afternoon trance and obey their inner voice.

How these drivers endure this weekly self-imposed torture is beyond me. They could quite easily leave later on Friday night or very early on Saturday morning to avoid this disaster of an escape strategy. However, just as much as these driving folk of Manhattan love their city all week long, they cannot wait until Friday to exit, and staying an extra few hours or one more night in the city simply isn't an option. So they drive for hours in their cars, stationary for much of it, cursing their decision to leave at the same time as hundreds of thousands of other drivers. But by the following Friday the very same drivers, having spent the whole week metaphorically living in their goldfish bowls, swimming aimlessly around and around, have no memory whatsoever of what has transpired each and every Friday since they were eligible to drive.

One way of cutting down on time spent in the car

is to invest in an E-ZPass, which is the electronic device that attaches to the windshield with Velcro and enables automobiles to pass through special toll lanes to get in and out of the city without lining up to pay cash. The driver still has to pay for the toll, but it is charged to their credit card instead, providing a minimum balance is maintained on that card for future toll use. Most New Yorkers have an E-ZPass since anything that saves time is generally welcomed.

So this begs the question, if it saves time and is no more expensive than paying cash, and assuming the potential user is of sound credit, why doesn't everyone have one? The problem with the E-ZPass is that it provides confirmation of one's whereabouts and can cause those up to no good to have the truth presented to them documented by E-ZPass records. Records are often subpoenaed for divorce trials and for those with travel restrictions imposed by the court who should not have ventured out of state. If paid for by work, they can provide useful information about individual staff playing hooky. Civil liberty advocates are completely opposed to the E-ZPass as it presents a documented example of Big Brother watching you. Hence those having extramarital affairs, those who are fleeing from the law, those skipping work duties, and those who distrust the government are the ones stuck in the cash lines entering the city. Thus never trust anyone who pays cash at the bridges and tunnels!

There is very little point in owning a really nice car in the city. In parking garages, cars get scratched and bumped in very tight spaces, and the undercarriage takes a severe beating on the uneven road surfaces and potholes. Many who own nice cars do so outside of the city and house them in much safer environments at their second homes. It is also rare to travel at a speed of greater than thirty to forty miles per hour within the confines of the city. Most of the time drivers experience stop-and-start driving with a very low average speed attained and dreadful fuel consumption. In some cases it is quicker to walk than drive. Sports cars are a rare sight indeed, especially those with manual gear transmission. Those who do dare drive a stick shift in the city suffer from a disease known as "sore right hand and overused left leg syndrome" caused by excessive clutch maneuvers and hand gear changes.

It can be extremely exhausting to drive in Manhattan both physically and, more importantly, mentally. You have to be focused at all times when driving and always aware of your surroundings. Anything and everything can invade your driving lane, from a slow-moving garbage truck that just changes lanes without signaling to a speeding Rollerblader equipped with headphones, who has no concept or regard for lane divisions or any other moving vehicle at all.

One of the more pleasurable moments for New Yorkers behind the wheel is usually enjoyed outside of the city on the return leg of a journey. Just as keen to leave the city for the weekend, especially in the summer months, residents of Manhattan cannot wait to get back. Two nights may not be a long time away from home for the average person, but for many a New Yorker this can seem like a life sentence. New Yorkers are, on occasion, hopeless at adapting to new environments and different ways of doing things. Being absent from the conveniences of Manhattan life causes much distress, since outside, the coffee tastes different, the newspaper isn't the same (even though it really is, with added sections), the service stinks, nothing gets delivered, and everything closes way too early. So, on the drive back into the city there are certain vantage points on the road where off in the distance you can just make out the skyline of Manhattan. It is at this exact moment, knowing that one is in striking distance of returning home, that New Yorkers become enveloped by a warm sensation, a moment of exultation and contentment. It can best be described as a return to the womb experience for New Yorkers who, on seeing the glorious skyline that represents everything about New York City, once again feel the security of returning to the cocoon that provides them with every creature comfort and high quality of life they know and cherish.

CHAPTER 12

Public Transportation

The vast majority of New Yorkers use services provided by the Metropolitan Transportation Authority (MTA) to meet their transportation requirements. Within Manhattan, this means hopping on a bus or stepping onto a subway train. What differentiates New York's public transportation system from most others in major cities is that the ticket price for a ride is based on single usage and not the length of the journey. So for the cost of a single ticket at $2.25, a user of the bus or subway can go anywhere in the five boroughs. The cost per mile is of incredible value to the rider, and even though the fare has increased 50 percent in ten years, it still represents the cheapest, most reliable, and in some cases, the cleanest form of transportation in the city.

The New York subway is the only subway system in the world that runs twenty-four hours a day, 365 days a year. Until Beijing finishes its own version, the subway system in New York City is the most extensive in the world, with over 660 miles of track. Every day of the year the New York subways carry more passengers than all the other American subway systems combined.

I love riding the buses in New York City. I particularly like the elongated buses with the stretchy elastic bit in the middle, since on the outside of these buses it looks like a giant concertina and inside there is a circle on the ground that rotates when the bus turns and provides riders with an extra thrill of twirling while en route. In London, to get more passengers on each bus they double up in size, height-wise. Thus there exists the term "double-decker bus." It takes up the same amount of room on the road as the single-decker but with almost double the amount of passengers. In New York the engineers decided to combine two buses length-wise, doubling the amount of space on the road the bus takes up. Space is one thing New York City does not have , and these buses are half a block in length. On a crowded bus, it can take a considerable amount of time to walk to the back of the bus as encouraged to by the bus driver. Passengers can walk their entire journey on board the bus.

The New York buses go up or down major avenues, with the exception of Park Avenue, and cross the city at major two-way cross streets, including several that intersect Central Park. There are many reasons given for the lack of buses on Park Avenue below 120th Street. The myth is that its wealthy residents have for decades resisted the use of noisy buses below them from their beloved Park Avenue apartments. There is no record of any all-powerful, super-rich Park Avenue activist lobby petitioning the city to ban buses on its prized avenue. One explanation is that flanking Park Avenue there is Lexington Avenue running from north to south and Madison Avenue running from south to north, with buses running on both these avenues making the need for buses on Park null and void. However, this makes no sense either as there are buses on York, First, Second, Third, and Lexington on the Upper East Side without a break. The most logical explanation is that from Grand Central Station until 97th Street, the Metro-North railway track runs underground Park Avenue with a distinct lack of reinforced concrete atop the tunnel to the street level, making the avenue sound hollow. This explains the loudness of the trains heard from low-level apartments on Park Avenue, as well as the lack of buses whose heavy pounding would one day land many of them on the tracks down below. If the myth about no buses on Park were true, wouldn't you think these rich, all-powerful, and influential folk would have somehow diverted the far noisier trains?

Traveling by bus allows the passenger to stay above ground for the entire duration of the journey, providing the bus doesn't get swallowed up by a giant pothole. The mere fact that you don't have to go underground to travel and can remain exposed to daylight means that happier people take buses. Bus passengers are also generally not in as big of a hurry as subway users because bus journeys do take longer, as the buses are exposed to standard traffic conditions. The bus lanes that flank the main avenues are often clogged by double-parkers or police patrol cars trying to enforce the bus lanes.

Catching a bus is also a more orderly procedure

than waiting for a subway train. Passengers line up in straight lines on the sidewalks at designated stops. Their place in line is by convention a reserved boarding spot, and even though many leave their place to partake in certain bizarre bus waiting practices, they are always able to return to their spot. Passengers waiting for their bus tend to bend their bodies forward so that their heads can peer over the sidewalk onto the street and direct their eyes to where the bus is coming from. Pass any bus stop in Manhattan and you see hoards of bus passengers involved in this strange contortion ritual of trying to locate buses in the distance. Many actually leave the sidewalk and step into the road to better ascertain when the bus is coming. The danger they put themselves through to find out information ahead of time is really rather futile. The driver doesn't speed up his vehicle because he sees a bunch of passengers stepping into the road gazing longingly at him from the next stop. Instead his main concern is not to hit one of the passengers in the street as he approaches them. I have witnessed passengers waiting in line having made a last-minute adjustment to get back onto the sidewalk in time for the arrival, only to misjudge and get swiped by a rather large wing mirror that clocks them in the head as the bus pulls up parallel to the sidewalk.

New York City buses are most used to cross town. The subway system was built primarily to ferry commuters in from the outer boroughs to Manhattan and to run in a general north to south direction once on the island. The main east to west subway artery runs from Penn Station to Grand Central and back again, better known as the S or shuttle train. It is the simplest and most efficient way of getting across midtown. Anywhere else too far north or south of Forty-second Street, the crosstown bus is a better plan. The problem is that everyone knows that this is the way to go, and the mere concentration of people being dropped off by other buses and subways at these crosstown hubs far exceeds the supply of buses available to transport them and the room on the streets for them.

One can use the intersection of Seventy-ninth and Lexington Avenue as a prime example of this buildup of human fodder in search of transportation. The Upper East Side has a large concentration of hospitals and many of its staff commute from outside of the neighborhood. They arrive at Seventy-ninth and Lexington from out-of-city express buses and from city buses coming in from Washington Heights and Harlem. They also arrive from Brooklyn, the Bronx, and downtown via the number 6 local subway. They all alight at roughly the same spot in need of a crosstown bus to transport them the final four blocks to work.

During rush hour, hundreds of folk line up awaiting the bus from the West Side. The bus arrives and deposits many who have crossed town to get to the East Side subway line. Once they have all gotten off, then the new passengers can step on, slide in their MetroCard, and make their way to the back of the bus to allow even more folk on at the front. The whole process takes about fifteen minutes, leaving those already on the bus upset with the newly boarded passengers, who in turn are angry for having had to endure waiting in line for a bus to come and then patiently wait to board a crowded bus full of moaning passengers. And finally there are the stragglers, who are rejected by the bus driver since the bus is stuffed full to capacity.

The city came up with the bright idea of apportioning more buses to alleviate the problem, which you would think would ease the crowding and cut back on turnaround time. Not so. These buses are so long you can't fit more than one at a bus stop, so not only do they not solve the existing problems that affect passengers but add the additional burden of clogging up junctions for cars and buses traveling in a perpendicular direction, creating an even bigger mess.

The buses do have a superior machine for swiping a MetroCard and accepting a fare. It is a vertical swipe machine as opposed to the horizontal and somewhat temperamental subway one. On the bus if the card doesn't work, you are at the mercy of the bus driver who with thirty other people waiting to board will more often than not wave you through free of charge.

That would not be the case on the subway. If the machine rejects the card then it's a choice of jumping the turnstile, with the threat of a long jail term if caught by the MTA police, or buying another card. In many subway stations, the electronic machine that vends new cards and tops up old ones is the only method of purchasing a fare. The cubicles that used to house fare-handling MTA staff are usually boarded up with a sign saying: "Please use the machines." The cutting of costs has almost reduced the human face of the MTA on the subway down to zero. Machines are cheaper to employ and don't need benefits, and in some cases are more productive than their human alternatives. As a result the only viable method of payment at the subway turnstile is a card, whether it is Metro or single ride, and these are perfect candidates for vending machines to distribute.

Coins are still a viable method of payment at the point of entry on a bus. For nine quarters deposited in the machine next to the driver, a fare to ride the bus is easily obtained. But don't try paying for a bus ride with a dollar bill. That, as far as the MTA is concerned, is sacrilege.

Most vending machines worldwide take bills as a form of payment. The MetroCard machine at subway stations takes them, as do drinks and candy machines dotted around the city. Yet New York buses haven't installed technology that can accept dollar bills. Coins and MetroCards are the only forms of payment available. Many tourists to the city are unaware of the no-dollar bills policy on New York buses. Visitors understand an exact change policy, but that it discriminates against what type of domestic currency can be used is a bitter pill to swallow. Every day scores of would-be bus users are denied a ride by bus drivers who turn them away for having two single dollar bills and a quarter. It's the right fare but the wrong texture of money.

There are many reasons for this policy. Apparently buses are more likely to be robbed if they contain dollar bills rather than a bunch of change, even though the amount of money being stolen is likely to be the same. Thieves in New York City obviously prefer bills to coins, as the latter slows them down on their getaway.

The finger is also pointed at the bus drivers themselves. They are not trusted to transport dollar bills from the bus to the accounts department at the bus depot. They are, however, entrusted to carry a metal lockbox full of quarters, nickels, and dimes. The truth is, the method of payment on buses needs to modernize. Passengers should be able to swipe credit cards, debit cards, and MetroCards and use dollar bills as well as coins. Taxis have recently woken up to change and permit credit card usage and buses need to follow suit.

Careful storage of a MetroCard is of paramount importance. The subway swiping machine to gain entry to the subway is very sensitive to any change in the shape of the card, and the slightest bit of damage can cause tremendous amounts of aggravation for the passenger. A card with a tiny dent in it will not swipe properly, but instead of informing the cardholder immediately that access is impossible, the machine will display a note saying "Please swipe the card again at this turnstile." The passenger will continue to perform this request and the turnstile swipe will carry on displaying the same message until a stalemate is reached. The passenger refuses to swipe anymore, usually because he has attempted so many times that his hand hurts, and the turnstile machine won't permit access, even if the card is stashed full of money. The aggrieved customer will then try another turnstile with similar results, before giving up on using the card successfully.

The passenger is then faced with a dilemma. He can either buy a new card and deal with the faulty one at a later date, or get in line to speak to an employee in the kiosk at major subway hubs if one is available. The dialogue with the employee once you arrive at the kiosk window will be brief. You will explain that the card doesn't work and that you have money on it. The employee will then take the card, briefly examine it, and try to swipe it in a machine. It won't work, of course, and the MTA employee will tell you that it is damaged, return your card, and attend to the next customer. So if that passenger wants to take the subway, he will have to buy a new card and store it in a better place than a back pocket or any place with a propensity to bend or dent or scratch it.

The best way of getting a refund is to contact the MTA directly outside of a subway station and follow the exact instructions. Avoid subway kiosks as much as you can unless all the machines are broken and you have no choice but to interact with a human. It's not that all subway MTA staff are rude, unfriendly, or incompetent. They are not. Simply put, they spend one-third of their life underground without any sunlight and have to deal with irate, frustrated, and disrespectful customers. You try to put on a smiling face every day and go to work happy putting up with these types of working conditions!

The lucky passengers who get through the turnstiles without any aggravation are treated to one of the finest subway systems in the world. It may not be modern: the subway cars are not particularly luxurious, and the facilities at the stations are on the whole archaic. In many stations, the subway trains share the tracks with the large population of Manhattan rats that live deep down underground, feasting on garbage left behind by passengers. However, what makes the subway so fantastic is that it is the quickest mode of transportation, it is mostly reliable and frequent, it is comparatively safe, and it extends across the whole of New York City. More people use the subway than any other form of transportation and this number increases during gridlock periods.

From just before Thanksgiving until after the New Year, the roads of Manhattan and all the approaches are jam-packed with holiday shoppers eager to descend on the exclusive stores of Manhattan. Throw in a Thanksgiving parade, holiday parties, end-of-year theatre shows for friends and family, the lighting of the tree at Rockefeller Center, and all the other Christmas and Chanukah light shows, and you have the recipe for complete mayhem and overcrowding above ground. Buses grind slowly through the streets, cars never move, and taxis are impossible to find. If you want to move around Manhattan between late November and early January head underground and use the subway. The subway cars may be more crowded and you will at times resemble a sardine stuffed into a rather small tin, but it is the only way of ensuring an on-time arrival achieved with a speed greater than walking pace.

Perhaps the most challenging part of riding the New York City subway is making sense of the announcements made on the loudspeaker at subway stations. What usually happens is that there is a crowded platform with no sight of a subway train approaching. The preannouncement piercing shrill of feedback causes distress to the ears of passengers eagerly awaiting travel information. Following this is a completely garbled announcement said rapidly as a train approaches on the opposite platform—it is impossible to decipher or hear. The only words the passenger can make out are "for those passengers traveling southbound on the . . . " Following the announcement, a rare interaction of complete strangers takes place. Normally eye contact on a subway train is completely taboo and is likened to stalking and sexual harassment. Passengers go to great lengths to avoid each other. You could be crammed into a subway train, body to body pressed next to one another, swaying and grinding with the motions of the train. Bodily parts intertwine and compete for any free space. It can have the appearance of simulated sex without eye contact since looking at another passenger would be an admission that bodily interaction had occurred, and could cause complete embarrassment or even worse: conversation.

After the garbled announcement, everyone is looking at each other for an explanation of what was transmitted over the speaker. All you see up and down the platform are confused passengers shrugging their shoulders in recognition that they are clueless to even partially understanding the information that has been broadcast to them. Eye contact is briefly attained along with limited conversation. Phrases such as "I have no idea" or "I didn't understand a word" are common conversation starters among those waiting. However, anyone who continues a conversation not relevant to the loudspeaker announcement or the lack of a train approaching is quickly avoided and finds himself alone on the platform, relegated to the status of lunatic or predator.

The New York subway system has done a sterling effort in cleaning itself up in the last two decades. Gone are the cars with offensive and heavy graffiti and hostile gangs beating up defenseless grannies. No longer are Guardian Angels in their bright red uniforms needed to defend innocent subway riders against the aggression of mindless thugs. Instead, the MTA police are visible on subway cars and at stations, and the public generally feels more assured and doesn't fret while riding the subway. This doesn't mean that crime has been eliminated completely from the subway: incidents do occur, but rarely are they headline material.

Many passengers take necessary precautions when riding the subway. Purses are zipped up and wallets are not openly displayed protruding out of back pockets. Crime prevention is extended to a whole group of engaged or married women who perform a sensible yet strange ritual before descending down into a subway station. They don't remove prominent rings with luscious, eye-opening gemstones. Instead they bizarrely turn the ring around so that the gem is inverted, facing inward rather than outward. All that is visible to the potential ring thief is the thin metal nongemmed section. It is a wise thing not to attract attention to expensive jewels in a public place like a subway car, and turning the gemstone around is considered by most women to be a sensible policy, but it really isn't a deterrent to a would-be thief. Wealth and decadence have a way of revealing themselves even without the display of an expensive ring. The hairstyle, the type of coat and clothing, the shoes, the makeup, the type of purse, the designer sunglasses, the manicured hands, and the five-carat diamond earring in each ear don't exactly help in deflecting attention. The phrase "If you've got it, flaunt it" isn't ideal for subway use and should be negated by more than just rings.

CHAPTER 13

Life as a Pedestrian

Manhattan is just as much a walking city as Paris and London. Many of its inhabitants walk to work on a daily basis and because of everything being in such close proximity, the need for a car or public transportation is lessoned somewhat. In most cases, it is possible to walk from your home or place of work to a supermarket/convenience store, a restaurant, a bank, a school, and a college. The sidewalks are wide and clean, and by and large the distance between each block from street to street is long enough to enjoy a leisurely stroll. Walkers on Fifth Avenue and Central Park West, if they journey on the Central Park side of the street, can have uninterrupted strolls for several blocks until a park cross-street intersection is reached. For those interested in gauging how far they walk in a day, the general formula is that twenty blocks up or down an avenue is a mile.

The city has been designed so that it is fairly easy to navigate the streets at crosswalks. Even numbered streets travel perpendicular to the avenues with traffic

going from west to east. Odd numbered streets are designated east to west. Of course, there are a number of
exceptions to this rule, which can confuse the pedestrian who has becomes accustomed to looking in different
directions for traffic at each intersection. An example
of one of these exceptions occurs in the fifties and sixties near the Fifty-ninth Street Bridge on the East Side.
Here, it is possible to witness pedestrians walking from
the sidewalk into the street, looking the wrong way,
hearing a loud honk of a horn, quickly turning their
heads to face oncoming traffic, and then scurrying back
to safety dodging certain death.

Walks along city streets can be hazardous, and jaywalking is never advisable. It is not illegal, since part of
the problem is that it poses huge troubles for observant
Jews on the Sabbath who cannot use electronics on that
day, and therefore cannot press the buttons needed to
activate some pedestrian crossings. The city realizes that
it can't have hoards of observant Jews waiting for long
periods of time on the sidewalks by crossings. They
will not break the Sabbath and so they simply wait for
a non-Jew to come along and press the button. What
would transpire at this point would involve the non-Jew
approaching the intersection and seeing loads of people waiting, and of course assuming that the button had
been previously pressed. He too then waits on the sidewalk for a long period without knowing what is happening. Therefore, observant Jews on Saturdays definitely
jaywalk more than any other ethnic group.

Jaywalking is frowned upon by law enforcement
since it clogs up traffic at the intersections. It is hard

enough dealing with motorists who don't adhere to logical and sensible traffic laws, and if you add in selfish pedestrians, it is no wonder that traffic comes to a complete standstill in Manhattan several times each day.

During rush hour periods, pedestrian traffic builds up in and around major transportation hubs like Penn Station and Grand Central Station. Photographed from above, pedestrians would resemble ants marching in and out of a colony. The pace of life in Manhattan is best witnessed by the speed at which its inhabitants and workers move around on foot. The pace is simply staggering. Crowds form at intersections where the sequence of lights prevents the pedestrian from crossing, but as soon as the light changes from stop to walk, two sets of pedestrians facing each other from opposite sidewalks jockey for position to enable them to cross as quickly as possible while avoiding head-on collisions in the middle of the street.

The convention of which side of the sidewalk a pedestrian should walk follows the convention of which side of the street the cars travel. Hence in most of the world, pedestrians should walk on the right-hand side and overtake on the right, with slow movers walking slightly right but to the middle. But, as with cars, pedestrians don't always follow the rules and overtake on the left if faced with slow-moving pedestrians ahead. When you add in the Commonwealth crew living in or visiting New York, who drive and walk on the left, it can cause a complete breakdown in walking etiquette. Many a time two pedestrians will meet head-on and do a rather silly dance trying to establish who should walk where. Some of the dances last for several seconds until the pair work out who should walk where, and they both move on without fuss.

If you happen to be walking at 6:00 p.m. on a weekday heading uptown from Grand Central Station, you resemble a salmon swimming upstream against the current. Ahead of you are thousands of commuters who work just north of Grand Central, rushing toward you trying to make their train departures to transport them back on time into the suburbs for the night. The pace at which they walk is breathtaking. The missing of a train that departs like clockwork so disrupts the commuters' schedule that they take no prisoners in their quest for punctuality. They hustle, run, barge, and push others out of their path and pay no consideration to pedestrians walking straight toward them. That is, unless a pedestrian walking toward them is singing really loudly while listening to headphones, clearing crowds as he walks. Since I walk north every weekday from Grand Central Station to get home, the clearing effect has kind of worn off, as the same people who used to voluntarily make a path for me now realize that after twelve years, I have yet to lash out or molest anyone and so close ranks. So I now often find myself either doing silly dances with the flood of commuters stampeding toward me, or just walk in the street so as to avoid being knocked over. I sometimes think being hit by a car might be more pleasurable than being bowled over by a commuter trying to catch a train.

Pedestrians have the right-of-way when the light is in their favor, even if a car is turning into a side street or onto an avenue. Providing a man lit up in white rather than red is displayed in front of them in the crossing light, then the pedestrians are free to cross. Be warned: Motorists in New York City do not understand this very simple code of conduct. A green light to the motorists means go, no matter what, even if they are turning. They rarely stop to let those on the sidewalks cross. The drivers nudge their cars forward, intimidating the pedestrians to hurry their crossing, and in some cases the motorists simply put their foot down on the gas while heavily beeping, forcing the pedestrians to stop in their tracks.

When walking the streets of Manhattan you put your life in your own hands every one-twentieth of a mile. If you walk at a pace of three miles an hour, you arrive at an intersection every minute for the entire duration of your walk with the Angel of Death hovering over your head. If you make it safely across, he accompanies you to the next one. The safest way to walk in Manhattan is to walk around the block, turning right as you leave your building and turning right a further four times at the intersections, assuring safe passage back to whence the walk started without ever crossing a street. You would have completed a perfect square. Providing you mainly have nowhere to go and you only visit friends who live on this route, it is unlikely that you will be killed by a car turning. Unless, of course, it oversteers and thus overcompensates its turn in order to prevent the car from hitting other pedestrians crossing and comes hurtling toward you on the sidewalk. This square-walking advice should not be heeded by pedestrians who live on blocks with parking garages because the likelihood of them being hit by a car increases dramatically, as cars can turn in and out of the garage midblock.

PART 3

Raising Kids and Pets in the City

CHAPTER 14

Manhattan Kids

Children are normally a reflection of their parents, and many behavioral traits, including speech, are picked up by the children because of the time spent with their parents. The same is true about Manhattan kids, except that many have the added factor of a nanny. My kids still to this day pronounce words the same way our nanny does. Rice Krispies are "rice kripsies," and "I don't want none of that" rather than "I don't want any of that" are common words and phrases in our household. The wrong pronunciation of a word and misuses of grammar are not serious crimes and we mostly let them go. The children will grow out of all of these phrases. What interests me is the amount of time Manhattan kids spend away from their parents and with their nannies so that they pick up these phrases.

Many families in New York need both parents to work to keep up with the high cost of living, but even in those families where there is a stay-at-home mom there usually is a nanny on hand. The nanny will do all the tasks that mothers don't like doing. The parents usually drop the kids at school, but nannies are the predominant pick-up choice at the end of a school day. Nannies take infants to music classes and gym time, where mothers and fathers are in the minority. Nannies also take the children on playdates and stay at the playdate apartment until it's time to go home. I have even seen nannies at places of worship on the weekend when the parents like to sleep in and the kids need to go to children's services. When I first took my eldest son to a children's service at a Manhattan synagogue, parents were in the minority. What was amazing to me was that the island nannies all knew the Hebrew songs, singing them word for word and clapping along while the kids who they were watching over aimlessly wandered around the room, oblivious to what was going on. Manhattan is certainly the only place on earth to witness Sabbath Hebrew songs sung gospel-style by babysitters of different faiths who are really into it.

There are many differences between kids who grow up in the suburbs and those who live in the city. Suburban kids have a lot more space inside their homes as they are more likely to grow up in a house as opposed to an apartment. Suburban kids can gain access, unsupervised, to outside space such as a backyard much easier than a city kid. In most cases, the backyard of city kids is Central Park, which they share with thousands of other kids at any one time. Suburban kids spend their life in a car being herded around for any activity. Families in the suburbs never walk, as in many towns sidewalks are absent. Even the most mundane task, such as fetching milk, requires the use of an automobile. City kids walk everywhere. They walk to the parks, they walk to the shops, and they are more likely to walk to school and almost all activities, including friends' homes and restaurants. City kids are more likely to leave their home for the weekend to a different home or a visit to the suburbs to see family and friends.

Suburban folk always harp on about how difficult it is to raise a kid in the city, and that argument is used as an excuse for moving out time and time again. It is certainly more expensive to live in Manhattan than outside. In the suburbs, accommodations are cheaper, education is cheaper, groceries are cheaper, and property maintenance is lower. The standard of living is also higher in the suburbs with more open spaces, less living on top of each other, and a better air quality to breathe. However, when one looks at the quality of life argument, there is a huge swing of the pendulum back to city life and in particular Manhattan. Those parents who commute do so at their own peril and spend hours on trains, on buses, and in cars getting into and out of the city. City parents can be back at home with their kids far faster than suburban ones, and can eat dinner with their children on most nights rather than just on the weekend. City kids don't spend their whole lives being transported in a car to see other friends and family and go to the mall. City kids walk to the movie theatre, visit parks often, and can be at a museum or theatre with the help of a short taxi ride. City kids live a more exciting life and tend to spend more time with both their parents.

I always argue that if the majority of those people who move out of the city once they have one child could stay in a larger apartment with enough living space and enough money to support their lifestyles in the city, they would never leave. The divorce rate isn't higher in the city, the obesity levels are lower in the city because everyone walks, the number of child suicides isn't higher in the city, and drug and alcohol use by the youth is just as likely in the city as in the suburbs. My wife and I are raising four kids in Manhattan, and yes, there are challenges. At times I could pull what little hair I have left out of my head, and my wife sometimes wants to pull my hair out too (not out of frustration with Manhattan but because it would hurt me). When frustration reaches a crisis point in our apartment, we always find something to do in the city: a bike ride in Central Park, a visit to a museum, out to dinner in a neighborhood restaurant, a visit to the paint-your-own-pottery place, a ride on a bus, a walk to a movie theatre, or a trip to many of the dog runs dotted around the city.

My suburban friends are the first to comment that city kids tend to be more confident, worldly, and outgoing. Kids in Manhattan are subjected to a whole plethora of nationalities, colors, religions, and cultures. Many suburbs are one-dimensional in terms of who lives there. There are WASPY towns, minority towns, Jewish towns, and Italian, Polish, and German towns outside in the suburbs. Manhattan isn't so much a melting pot, which describes the meshing of many cultures into one predominant one; instead it is more of a tossed salad where a tomato can live in close quarters with a radish and a lettuce leaf and be comfortable being tossed around all day in a small bowl without any conflict.

Manhattan opens up kids' eyes to so many different cultures. On the same block you can have a mosque, a synagogue, a Hindu temple, and a church without batting an eyelid at their close proximity. An ultra-Orthodox Jewish man in full garb passes a Seventh-Day Adventist on the way to prayer as the Sabbath comes in, walking just in front of a devout Muslim returning from Friday prayers, and no conflicting thoughts enter any of their heads. Manhattan kids see these types of scenarios all the time. It is very different from being in a cookie-cutter-type home in the suburbs with everyone of similar mentality, driving the same car, going to the same school, and eating out at the same local spots.

CHAPTER 15

The Manhattan Nanny

By far the biggest end-of-year tip or bonus gets handed out to the nanny or babysitter. The convention is to tip the person who spends more time with your children than you do a week's salary. Every year my wife says to me, "You need to withdraw money for the babysitter's bonus," and I always can only retort with a begrudging, "Ouch." I then pinch myself and bring myself back to reality quickly since the voice of my late father tends to echo inside my head for rather long periods. He was a great believer in the theory that if someone works in your household you have to treat him like family. Think about this: What is the upside of having a bad relationship with someone you entrust your children's welfare to every working day? There is none. So with this thought in mind, the bonus paid to our babysitter every year-end is probably the best money I spend each year.

The other day I introduced our babysitter to a friend as, "This is our nanny." Apparently I completely offended her as she corrected me midsentence and said, "Hi, actually I am the babysitter." Apparently there is a huge difference between a nanny and a babysitter in the child-caring world in New York City. I had no idea. There doesn't appear to be a social stigma attached to being a nanny compared to being a babysitter, so the only logical explanation is that babysitters get a higher hourly rate than nannies. After consulting with fellow babysitter employers and a few who claim to have nannies, I have found this to be true. For this book's purposes, I treat the terms the same and interchange them so as not to offend anyone.

There seems to be very little logic in determining how child care should be compensated. The other area of confusion for me seems to be a discrepancy in pay between babysitters who live in and those who arrive promptly every morning but who go home at night after a day's work. The latter are more highly paid, especially in hourly terms. The live-in nannies/babysitters are paid less because accommodations and meals are provided for by the employer, five days a week. Yet they still need a place to stay during the weekend when they are off work, and the last time I checked, unless you stay in a hotel, most accommodations in the tristate area are based on signing a lease, which at a minimum is monthly, making paying for accommodations a moot point. However, the day babysitter usually works a ten-hour period from 8:00 a.m. to 6:00 p.m. and can eat breakfast, lunch, and sometimes dinner with the kids, also provided for by the employer. So in reality, live-ins are cheaper because if the babysitter has her own family she will want to see them occasionally, and so anyone willing to sacrifice her whole week to be with another family should be paid less. I still don't get it. I believe the pay structure should be the other way around. I am sure these observations now mean I am a target of both live-in employers as well as non-live-in babysitters.

In choosing child care for one's kids in New York major decisions have to be made in advance. Will you hire an "illegal nanny"? The term reflects those who have entered the United States legally but who have outstayed their tourist visa and are forbidden to work here. If you are a public official or you intend to run for office one day, I would not recommend your hiring in this category. This can come back to haunt you. Once a decision has been made about the legality of the nanny's immigration status, the next dilemma is whether to pay her on or off the books. Obviously the cost to the employer is greater if the nanny is paid strictly in cash and off the books, and many in the city choose this option since child care is expensive enough as it is. Be aware that this is also illegal and that if you employ an illegal nanny you may have two agencies knocking at your door looking for back payment and fines. That would be the INS and the IRS. Since 9/11 and the global recession these are two agencies that are both on a mission, and the risks of getting caught have increased dramatically. The little extra money of placing an employee on the books and filing quarterly tax forms with the IRS far outweighs the risk of getting caught and all the consequences surrounding lawbreaking.

With this choice made, the next area to concentrate

on is what hours the nanny will help your family out: full time or part time? What will you pay per hour? How many weeks vacation will she get? What will you do about sick days? What are her daily chores? First-time nanny employers in New York City can get over-whelmed by the whole process, as they don't have a human resources booklet for guidance to help them hire the right person with the proper job description, including benefits. It is best to have an idea about where your priorities lie and which responsibilities of the babysitter are deal breakers well before the search starts to fill the vacancy. There are babysitters who won't cook; won't clean; won't look after more than two kids; won't come in before 7:00 a.m.; won't stay after 5:00 p.m.; won't do pickups from school; won't change dirty diapers; won't clear up tables or toys; won't do laundry; won't discipline the kids; won't take checks for payment; won't come in on holidays you have never heard of; and so on. With some interviews, an employer wonders what these nannies do all day long apart from devise a list of what they won't do.

The responsibilities of nannies vary with the age of the kids they are looking after. When kids reach school age, nannies spend a lot of time on their own in your home, and if you want to keep them you still have to pay them to do less and less each year. Yet, if both parents are working, kids need to be taken to school, collected, and babysat until a parent returns home from work. Please never stop and think that you are paying a nanny to watch daytime soaps every day, even though that is what many do since the cleaning up and preparing for the arrival home of all in the household covers just the first hour of each day.

Manhattan nannies are a different breed of day-care providers. They arrange their own playdates for themselves, which the kids who they are looking after happen to come along to. They eat out in restaurants with money from their employers. Nannies tend to stick together along ethnic and national lines. Those from Guyana have their own club. Jamaicans stick together. The Filipino nannies are all chummy with one another. Each nanny group is a reflection of language differences and cultural similarities. Even though English is the common denominator among all nannies, Spanish speakers are dominant, primarily from Central and South America, and many dialects of English can be heard from the different nanny communities. Often employers will insist on fluent English speakers but find it a bonus if their children can pick up a second language without having to pay for private tutors. South American families tend to hire Spanish speakers. French speakers hire from the French-speaking islands and English-speaking couples are more susceptible to employing those from the islands where English is the first language. The Filipino nannies are for some reason the most in demand since they have a reputation of being the hardest working, most conscientious, and least troublesome in the workplace.

Nannies talk and gossip a lot among each other, and employers pry their own nannies for information about other families and other nannies. Whatever goes on within the four walls of your home expect another family to hear about it almost instantaneously. Nannies are fantastic in broadcasting the latest news, and if you don't want your dirty washing hung in public, get rid of the nanny, quit work, and raise your kids yourself. Nannies are the first to know about imminent divorces, they pick up on behavioral problems of other kids, and know whether or not the wife or husband is involved in extracurricular activities. Remember: When you let someone into your home, and inevitably into your life, and they spend a huge amount of time witnessing what goes on at home, it is likely to be spoken about in someone else's company.

New York nannies are savvy businesswomen. They are tremendous at holding their employers to ransom over pay and benefits, and even during a recession when households are cutting back as a result of reduced compensation, the nanny somehow is able to secure a pay raise above the rate of inflation. Households that have employed the same nanny for years are so frightened of losing her that many of the mothers negotiate pay behind their husband's back in fear of being berated by their spouses. Nannies can earn $17–$20 an hour working in the city. That is well above the minimum wage, and rates have not come down at all with the latest downturn in the economy. Mothers would rather get rid of their husbands than dispose of their nannies, and unfortunately the nannies know this. There are of course exceptions to the rule with certain employers operating a revolving door to their home. The employers who hire and fire at will reflect the lack of patience or judgment of many a household in the city. These families have to pay a higher premium to entice a nanny to come and work with them, as employers' bad reputations are pretty much public knowledge.

First-time nanny hunters are always on the prowl looking for prospective hires. When pregnant with child, they tend to hover around children's playgrounds and other city nanny hangouts. They observe nannies' behavior with the kids they are looking after, and if they appear to be nurturing, warm, and affectionate, they approach them when no one is looking and offer them more money to leave their present employers. Armed with this ammunition nannies normally receive a pay raise from their current employer and secure job stability, and are considered honest for approaching their employer with their dilemma. New York City nannies don't need agents. They should all work on Wall Street or in the cutthroat advertising world.

CHAPTER 16

The Private School Admissions Process

There are some fantastic public schools in Manhattan, and some not-so-good ones. Rents and prices of apartments reflect whether the public school zoned to your building is beneficial or not. The gifted and talented programs offered and subsidized by the city are also fabulous, but are even more difficult to get into than private schools, since they offer top-notch education for free. If you choose the public school option, you save yourself and your spouse considerable aggravation and heartache.

However, if you aren't in a good public school district, and you are unwilling to move within the city or outside the city, then you will be considering private schools for your children. For some, the real process of trying to gain admission into one of these schools can start before the child is born. With parochial schools, preference is given to members of the affiliated Manhattan church or synagogue. If parents want to send their kids to one of these religiously affiliated schools, they normally join a place of worship when they get married with the intention of sending their child there. The nearer the time gets to the application process, the more these parents are likely to regularly attend services. Relationships are struck up with the clergy, parents start hanging around after services to introduce themselves to key staff, and donations to causes promoted by the church or synagogue increase dramatically. Manhattan parents are experts in working the system, and they think they are ingenious; that is, until they go to services on a Saturday or Sunday a few weeks before the admissions process begins and see the two hundred other families with toddlers sitting on their parents' laps, misbehaving and looking bored out of their minds. Realizing they were not as clever as they had previously thought, parents give each other a nod to show they understand why they are all there.

Demand for places in Manhattan private schools far exceeds supply. The choices include coed or single sex, parochial or nondenominational, East Side or West Side and downtown or uptown. Within each choice there are further choices: Catholic or Presbyterian, Orthodox Judaism or Reform Judaism, or somewhere in-between. Widening the choices increases the chances of getting accepted, while closing the doors on a particular school because of a less-than-desirable geographical location within Manhattan affects a child's chance of getting in somewhere.

The odds of getting into the school of your choice are lowered even further by a sibling policy that puts meritocracy to shame. Apart from real behavioral-problem children, a sibling is almost guaranteed a place in the same school where the older brother or sister attends. This narrows down the number of places available each year to newcomers. In coed schools, the sibling acceptance policy can weigh heavily in favor of or against one gender if all the siblings wishing to enter are almost all girls or boys. I remember going on an interview for my eldest daughter with the head of admissions, who told my wife and me that the school needed eleven boys and one girl that year. I felt like saying, "Thank you so much for bringing us in today for this pointless exercise," but restrained myself in case all heads of admission talk to one another, with particular focus on psychopathic fathers. My daughter did not get into this school, so as a result neither did my next two children.

To infuriate parents even more, each school charges a fee for the application process. It ranges between $50 and $100 per application, with small reductions in some cases for twins or triplets. (Placing one child is hard enough and a full-time project on its own. I can't even imagine what it is like when more than one is involved.) The application process costs several hundred dollars and takes hours and hours of meticulous planning and strategy. It is exhausting and stressful, and becomes a real nail-biter the closer the calendar moves toward DecisionDay, when the acceptance letters, and, in some cases, phone calls go out about six months after the process started.

The process of getting a first-born child into a private school in Manhattan is reason enough to leave this otherwise terrific city and head for the hills. Here is our story: We missed the cutoff zone for a really good public school by about five feet, and the city wouldn't budge on rezoning or relocating my kids. I therefore knew at the outset that we either had to move apartments, send them to a less-than-adequate public school, or go private. I consulted with my wife; she is a product of public school education in New Jersey, who I thought would lean toward the public option, considering how well she was educated. How wrong I was. It was private school in the city for all our kids, or she would find another husband. Being quite fond of her, private school it was.

The admissions process started when I was relaxing at home on Labor Day Monday with my then two-year-old daughter. I was told that I needed to make myself available the next day at 9:00 a.m. I was confused why I needed to be on call at a crucial time of my morning at work. My wife informed me that this was the exact time the phone lines opened to either put ourselves down on a highly interested list, or to order an application form from the private schools we were interested in. We had previously discussed which schools we were interested in, and had eliminated the schools we had no chance whatsoever of gaining acceptance to or whose philosophy was so diametrically opposed to everything we believed in that we couldn't send our child there.

Nine schools were in contention to be fortunate enough to offer my daughter a place. On the Tuesday after Labor Day, I went to work armed with the incredibly valuable ammunition of five phone numbers to register my daughter for an application form or secure a date to come in and tour the various schools. I was given more phone numbers than my wife, because she correctly ascertained that my work phone system was marginally quicker with the redial function. So on that Tuesday morning, one senior managing director at a United States investment bank dealing in hundreds of millions of dollars, had to put all trading and financial transactions on hold until five administrators from Manhattan schools became well versed in my daughter's name, age, and address.

I tried to sneak in a couple of calls at two minutes to nine to try to outsmart the system, but received a busy tone suggesting others had tried this tactic too. At nine on the dot, I borrowed my colleague's phone on the desk and started dialing two numbers at once. Both were busy. I pressed redial for both and got an unexpected: "This telephone number is not in working order." I pressed redial again for both and received the message: "Due to network congestion, I am afraid we cannot connect your call. Please dial later." "Later" was five seconds for me. Busy again. I called my wife to see how she was progressing. Her line was busy too, so I called her cell phone. Janet picked up and said, "I hate this." I asked her if she had had any success so far. She hung up on me. I guess that meant no.

It was now 9:06 a.m. I was zero for five. Dial, busy, hang up, and redial. Dial: "No such number," hang up, and redial. Dial: "Network congestion," hang up, and redial. At 9:37 a.m., I got through on one of the two numbers, but I was so used to dialing, hearing a message, hanging up, and redialing that I hung up on the woman answering the phone at one of the schools. I quickly realized what I had done and pressed redial. Busy. So I did what any grown man would have done at this point: I smashed my head on the desk and kept on smashing it until my assistant asked me, "Is everything OK?" Aha, I thought. Four hands are better than two. "Here, dial this number and don't speak until you have someone on the line." So for the next ninety minutes the two of us dialed frantically until I had spoken to all five on my list, and had given my details and arranged dates to visit the schools.

I called my wife to tell her the good news while simultaneously e-mailing her the dates and times so that they would not conflict with those on her list. When Janet picked up the phone she started sobbing, rising to hysterical, uncontrollable tears. I wondered what could possibly have happened? Had my daughter been rejected before the rejection process had started? Were the schools all filled up with younger female siblings? I really couldn't get much of an answer, since her voice kept breaking up being interrupted by her vocal chords trying to reestablish calm. I told her to relax and take deep breaths, which she complied with. I then asked her to answer one simple question: "How many schools have you spoken to?" There was then complete silence for several seconds, followed by a very squeaky, mouse-like response: "None."

My wife had stopped calling after thirty minutes, and had reached the conclusion that it was impossible to get into any of the schools. I told her of my success, and so she suggested I call the last four myself, as I was so fantastic at it. I felt bad for her, and dutifully carried out the task up until completion. I had none of my wife's doom-and-gloom prognosis. I was optimistic that one school would realize that my daughter was a prime candidate for scribbling, finger painting, and crayoning for three hours a day at the cost of $20,000 a year.

We had thus secured our nine appointments. Five were open houses and four were meet-the-head-of-admissions-without-your-child type of meetings. For the next three months, we would spend several hours touring the schools and their facilities, and listen to teachers and principals tell us how wonderful their schools were. Also, we heard the sad news that there were very few places that year available to girls, as the city had seen an epidemic of sibling sisters.

The first open house was actually quite interesting. The curriculum, philosophy, and teaching methods of the school were explained to us in great detail and both my wife and I were diligently taking notes. There was a chance for questions at the end, and eight different parents asked questions whose answers were already alluded to in the tour (had they been listening, instead of spending most of their time devising questions). By the time the seventh person asked a question he already knew the answer to, I understood why people buy guns and either use them on others or use them on themselves. I am proud to say to this day I have never asked a single question in any school open day. I despise those who do. They are trying to get noticed, like the sound of their own voice, or were just born annoying. Most of the administrators have been doing this job for years.

There isn't a single question that hasn't been asked before, since everything about the open day is designed to cover all aspects of the school. The process is foolproof but attended by lots of fools.

So after the fourth open house, having seen lots of happy faces at the schools both at infant and teacher level, and having received an education in what three-year-olds actually do at nursery school, I was still confident that our daughter would get into one of our chosen schools. That was, until we were called in to meet the administrators face-to-face in a one-on-one question-and-answer session. Unlike the previous encounters in large rooms with eight sets of parents where we could blend into the finger-painting displays on the walls, we could now mess up our chances for our daughter in a whole host of ways. One wrong answer could jeopardize months of preparation.

These were very stressful times. My wife reminded me on the morning of the first interview that I really wasn't very funny and that I should refrain from trying to inject English humor into anything that I said. She also told me that she would answer the questions, because I was British and didn't know anything. I weighed up a suitable response to her put-down but realized that she had placed me in a win-win situation. If our daughter didn't get in, then I could blame my wife because I hadn't said anything. If my daughter got in because of this tactic, then happy times all round. She would then be in and I really didn't care who got her in as long as she was in. I actually couldn't have devised a better strategy myself. I didn't have to say anything at all: just show up in a nice suit and tie and shake hands, look interested, and smile occasionally.

I of course went along with my wife's plan, following it to a tee, and for the first three interviews I said nothing but "Nice to meet you," "Goodbye," and "Thank you." I was the almost perfect mute. I did get some strange looks from the interviewers who tried to steer the line of questioning toward me, but I was having none of it.

After the third interview, my wife turned to me and asked if I was completely or just partially retarded. I didn't understand the context of her line of attack, so I asked her to clarify. She explained that I hadn't uttered a single word in any interview, and that no school would even look at the daughter of a now-well-known psychopath. How could my plan have backfired so quickly? And why was it still my fault if my daughter got rejected, as I had followed my wife's advice so studiously? My daughter had attended five playdate-type interviews with my wife: these were the follow-ups to the open days and were designed to allow the selectors to do their job while observing the kids. According to my wife, all five had not gone well.

I know you are thinking to yourself that none of these could be blamed on me. I was, after all, not present at any of these interviews, so I should logically be in the clear. However, I was informed by my wife that the overall mood of the child on these observation days can be affected by something a father has done or said up to three days previous. I realized pretty soon that if my daughter failed to get into one of these schools, I was the scapegoat. That is when I took matters into my own hands, trying to reverse the tide.

We were attending the final interview on our schedule and my wife turned to me in the waiting room and said, "You had better speak this time. Do a good job or I will kill you. Our daughter's academic life depends on how you do." Therefore, armed with a green light, I put on my helmet, tightened my goggles, checked my boots and skis, and set off on the nursery school triple-black-diamond admission trail with one aim in mind: to get to the bottom of this huge mountain with my daughter accepted as one their students.

The door to the head of admissions' office opened, and a little old lady came out and extended a hand to both of us, ushering us into her sparsely decorated room. I detected a slight hint of a German accent when she introduced herself. We sat down in adjacent chairs opposite her desk. The first thing she remarked on was my distinct English accent, and inquired which part of England I was from. I took a small gamble and replied in German, asking her which part of Germany she was from. It worked. She stopped peering down at our application form and looked up beaming and grinning from ear to ear like the Cheshire cat. "You speak German?" she asked with a facial expression that longed for an affirmative answer. We then chatted for about fifteen minutes in free-flowing German, covering comparative education systems, European life versus life in America, and our respective family backgrounds.

My wife looked stunned. She had been completely carved out of the whole process and was sitting there speechless. The admissions head and I laughed and discussed and intellectually stimulated each other, until she abruptly brought the conversation to a halt. She turned to my wife and immediately changed the conversation back into English, asking her when she could bring what sounds like our delightful daughter in to be observed. "It's just a formality," she said. "As long as your child doesn't display any disruptive behavioral characteristics, she will have a place in the school." My wife and I looked at each other and embraced briefly and we profoundly thanked the lady for her time and effort.

This goes to show how the process is so arbitrary. You never know which issue will sway an admissions head one way or the other. For us, it was a command of the German language by one parent, and a chance for this woman of European origin to reminisce about her past. We were one of the lucky ones. Most parents have to wait months to find out if their child is accepted.

The playdate interviews for the children are pretty straightforward and are events that are very difficult to prepare for. Two-year-olds are unpredictable at the best of times and never perform when you want them to. Here are a couple of helpful hints: It is in a classroom full of toys and other kids, so don't put your sons in cute Ralph Lauren suits or your girls in pretty pink dresses. They will get trashed and you will look like a buffoon for doing so. Make sure they are comfortable in what they are wearing.

The various staff from the school observing are looking out for certain preordained traits in children.

They are the professionals. They are not expecting your child to be the perfect sharer or the most active child. Some kids are more intelligent than others and most schools are looking for a balanced classroom. They want quiet kids and noisy ones, boisterous ones and tepid ones, friendly ones and ones who go into a corner and play with one toy by themselves. There is no right or wrong child. Some kids are more independent and others never leave their parent's side. Only send one parent—it really doesn't matter which one. Admissions staff don't want to see overindulgence by the parents; neither do they want to see kids being ignored if they display violent tendencies. In some cases parents leave upset, thinking they won't get in after their kid had a tantrum while playing with a toy truck, and then a couple of months later they hear by e-mail that they have been accepted. Nobody has figured out the process yet.

The date for acceptances to go out is centralized as all schools have waiting lists. This is based on the fact that most children apply to multiple schools, and the schools are never aware of which is the first choice for parents. In interviews, parents tell each and every school that this is their first choice. Once you have an acceptance letter, parents have very little time to make up their minds. The process is fast, frantic, and mind-consuming. The lucky parents with more than one choice need to make a decision that day on where their child will be educated for nursery school and in many cases beyond. It is a mind-boggling experience and not for the faint-hearted or indecisive. Those who are only on the waiting list must do exactly that. They must wait. No phone call or bribe can get them moved up the list and the lack of information is frustrating. Families actually move out of the city each year because demand outstrips supply. Public schools outside of the city are viewed as superior to those in the city by parents who move out because of private school rejection. They also have a tendency to immediately start condemning New York City private schools once rejection turns into reality.

My eldest daughter gained acceptance to two schools and was wait-listed at three. We accepted the offer from the school that had already informally given us a place, and quickly rejected the other and removed ourselves from the waiting lists. It had been a very stressful process, but it was now over and we could move on to the next hurdle.

So now all my kids are in private schools. The big question is: Are the schools worth the money, or am I throwing money down the drain?

CHAPTER 17

How Much for Tuition?

The reality of private school fees sunk in when, two weeks after acceptance, we were sent a welcome pack from the school, together with a bill for $15,000 for one year's tuition for a three-year-old. My math background came in handy again. I estimated from the school calendar that my daughter would be in school for about one hundred and fifty days—that took into account vacations, sick days, public holidays, teacher development days, and parent-teacher conferences. She would be in school for three hours each day. That was $33 an hour. This was twice the cost of employing a nanny full-time for ten hours each day. I lost the argument about keeping her home with our nanny very quickly. So I wrote the check out begrudgingly to the school.

I did notice a box that could be ticked for financial assistance. I was pleased to see this, as I was a little concerned that my daughter would be attending school with a tiny cross section of society. The New York City private schools do offer assistance to those families who cannot afford tuition through either partial- or full-scholarship programs. The applicants are means-tested and thorough background checks are carried out to determine an ability to pay. Those who have little or no income but assets galore are also filtered out so that families living on Fifth Avenue in penthouse apartments with an entire staff but are unemployed out of choice will be excluded too. Approximately one-tenth of all families in private school receive some sort of assistance either from the school or from their own families. It adds a diversity of backgrounds to the school's makeup as well as giving the school a chance to give back to the community. All financial assistance is anonymous, so no one ever knows who is on the program and how much help they are getting.

The fees for private school increase per the number of hours your child attends each day. There is no set formula for setting the price. The school fees are pretty similar across the whole spectrum of schools in the city, and are double the amount you would pay for privately educating kids in the suburbs. By the time your child reaches eighth, grade, the fees currently run at $36,000 a year, so it is very important that you budget for this going forward. To bring home a sense of reality, for each child at a private school in a 50 percent tax bracket you need to earn $72,000 a year just to afford the fees alone. It doesn't stop there either.

As soon as the child starts school, you will be asked by the class teacher for a set contribution for the year's activities not covered by the school, such as cocktail parties and presents for the teachers and an end-of-year picnic. Yes, you have to contribute for a present to the teacher even before she has taught anything. That is the system. If you don't like it then don't send your kid to a private school. You will also be asked to contribute to the Parent Teacher Association, which is a tremendous organization and well worth supporting. They will ask for a donation early in the school year. A strong PTA usually means a great school too. Each school strives to become better each year and has to keep up with new innovations in the classroom, especially in the fields of technology and recreation. These items are not usually included in the school budget and so the PTA looks for generous contributions from the parents.

Then there is the building fund. Each school seems to have one as it appears that each school is bursting at the seams and needs to build upward, inward, and outward. I wouldn't want to be a neighbor of a school, since at any moment the building fund could arrive, threatening repossession and removal. Those on the building committee are particularly aggressive: they don't ever accept no as an answer and have no qualms about calling you at all hours of the day asking you to contribute. You eventually agree just to stop the phone calls. Don't even think of pledging and then not coming up with the money. The building committees have sub-collection committees whose members are even more ruthless and take no prisoners.

Add all of this to the annual campaign committee and the special events committee and the scholarship fund. You didn't think the school solely provides funds for scholarships? That isn't included in the budget, and the threat of increased school fees always looms if any of these committees don't reach their required target. So when you sign up for private schools and gain acceptance to one of them, don't budget just for school fees, as this isn't the case. Also, in case you were one who thought you could get away with just school fees, the school publishes in its annual report the names of all the donors to the various campaigns. If your family name isn't on the list then everyone starts talking about why you haven't given. You are either bankrupt, Scrooge-like, or dead. You don't want to be labeled any of these. Always give something. Remember to stay off the radar at all times.

The first meeting at the school for new parents occurs just after the new academic year starts in September. The event is normally held in a school hall or gym. The acoustics are dreadful, the food barely edible, and the wine could be used as a substitute for pickling cucumbers. The principal will give a talk and tell you to look around the room and see the people who will become your closest friends in years to come. Everyone always tells you that you become soul mates with the parents of your kid's friends, as you have so much in common with them. Single friends become scarce in your social calendar bookings, and those married folk who don't want kids are treated as if they are aliens. What is certainly true is that as time progresses, those friends with kids of similar age to your own will be sharing the same experiences and so are bound to have more in common with you than single or childless friends.

As I looked around the room that fateful night

of the introductory cocktail party, all I could think of was fifteen years of private school adds up to close to a half-million-dollar investment per child, and once I surveyed the whole room I concluded that I had never before seen such a concentration of social misfits in my entire life. I could not find one couple with whom I could talk. I couldn't find one dad whom I had anything in common with. I couldn't even find the dad who couldn't find one dad either. I laughed at the principal's speech and told my wife there was absolutely no chance of us being friendly with anyone there and not to ever make arrangements to go out with one of them unless I vetted the person properly. I was wrong, because seven years later, we have at least five couples that we are extremely close with and see socially on a regular basis.

CHAPTER 18

Dogs and Their Owners

The cramped living spaces and urban concrete sprawl of Manhattan would, at first glance, seem like an unsuitable environment for raising and keeping a pet, especially one that needs constant walking and extensive exercise to stay healthy. Animal lovers who don't know Manhattan would think it cruel to keep a dog indoors, cooped up in a small apartment all day while the owner is at work. Manhattan dog owners argue the complete opposite. They claim that dogs in the city are treated umpteen times better than those outside. They are pampered, walked, groomed, loved, and adored more than most humans. What is undeniable is that there are more cases of spousal and child abuse in Manhattan each year than there are cases of animal cruelty. Manhattan loves its dogs and provides privately owned facilities for them as well as public dog runs in most of the major recreational areas.

I have never owned a dog, but I have always wanted one. As a kid, my father, sister, and I tried to persuade my mother to have a family dog. She retorted with the ultimatum, "It's either the dog or me." So we deliberated for a few days before we informed my mother that by virtue of a slim majority we had decided to keep her and not purchase a dog. We never did tell her who the solitary vote for her was, but it wasn't me. I really wanted a dog. When I moved to New York City I saw dogs everywhere I went, and I thought long and hard about buying one for the family to play with and love. I thought it would be therapeutic, and to have unconditional love for something, which is reciprocated, was a further magnet pulling me ever closer toward dog ownership. So I suggested the idea to my wife.

"That is a fantastic idea," she said. "Why don't you research what breed you are looking for and how much it costs, and how long it will take to toilet train, and look into dog walking and grooming services too. Oh, and don't tell the kids either as I think you will probably disappoint them."

I knew what was coming next. I thought I was going to receive the usual lecture about my not doing anything to help out in the house, and that I would be at work when the dog needed to be walked, and that the kids needed to be in school early in the morning and she had the baby and the dog needed to be walked. I thought this would lead to a whole argument about taking the dog outside when it was cold and rainy. But all I could muster from these thoughts of imminent conflict was a rather wimp, weak, and asking-for-further-torment type of question:

"Why would I disappoint the kids?

"Because we live in a no-dog building, you fool," my wife responded looking fairly smug and victorious.

This was true. I had completely forgotten about that. In the house rules of our co-op building, dogs were not allowed. It had been voted on way back at an annual general meeting following an attack in the elevator by a yelping small dog on an elderly woman tenant returning from shopping. The vote in favor of the proposal to ban future dogs was passed overwhelmingly in sympathy with the little old lady who sat at the front of the meeting sobbing. All potential future dog owners who lived in our building or who wanted to move in with a dog had three choices: the first was to move out and own a dog in another building, the second was not to buy an apartment in our building because who wants to live in a building where the majority of the tenants are evil dog haters, and the third was to have a dog in the building and not tell anyone.

I know this last option seems ridiculous. The by-laws clearly stated that no dogs could be kept as pets in our building. That didn't mean that tenants couldn't dog-sit for a friend or have a family pet over to look after when the owners were on vacation. We had two tenants who dog-sat on what seemed like a full-time basis. When confronted by the board and the management company, both tenants stressed and argued vehemently that that they were dog-sitting and didn't actually own the dog. The board decided after three months of monitoring the situation, including checking the collars of both dogs and finding our building address displayed on them, that these dogs were permanent residents. The tenants were issued a polite request to remove the dogs as quickly as possible.

What transpired next was possibly the most bizarre series of events that I have seen or heard about in a Manhattan apartment building. The dogs went "underground" and into hiding. The owners never signed the form stating that they had removed the dogs from the building, but no one saw or heard the dogs for some time. The owners of these canines began to behave a little differently too. Tenants noticed that on many occasions when these tenants left the building, they did so with large baskets slung over their shoulders with lots of blankets atop. Doormen noticed that there was movement coming from below the blankets. Whereas before these tenants had always been super friendly to others, always letting kids pet their dogs as they slowly and casually walked with them through the lobby, they now sprinted from the elevator to the front door and out onto the street with not so much as a hello for anyone.

An extraordinary shareholders meeting was called by the board to confront this standoff between these couple wayward tenants and themselves. Threats of legal action hung in the air from both sides, and the tension between board and dog owners became visibly more strained. The day before the meeting, one of the dog owners caved in to the considerable pressure from the majority viewpoint in the building and decided to give her dog to her daughter, who was moving to the West Coast. The other dog owner dug in her heels and resisted others' calls to back down or compromise.

The meeting was probably the most highly attended

one that I could recall. The anti-dog brigade gave out leaflets, the moralists who defended co-op bylaws also leafleted, a couple of free speech proponents stood at the entrance to the church hall giving out First Amendment flyers, and the pro-dog lobby was there with ASPCA literature. One other tenant was giving out cards for her hat business. It was a free-for-all. The meeting was rowdy, confrontational, and fairly aggressive. Both sides argued their point of view, with the pro-dog lobbyists being booed by the other side when they spoke. The board finally conveyed through the lawyer from the management company that lawsuits would follow, as this was a serious breach of co-op law.

Ninety days went by, and the dog was no longer in the basket but instead paraded proudly through the lobby. The dog continued to stay in the building, and the status quo was actually quite manageable. The dog-owning tenant kept getting fines on her maintenance bills for blatantly abusing the building's constitution, and the board held meetings to discuss what to discuss at future meetings and whether they should hold meetings, and formed subcommittees to liaise with lawyers and other non-dog buildings' boards. Six months went by and still there was no resolution and no sign of any middle ground. Legal fees built up, and the number of board meetings and committees reached a frenzy. But amidst this chaos, everyone in the building, including the fiercest dog haters, got used to having one dog permanently there. My family loved the dog and its owner too. We were entrenched in keeping dog and owner here.

Then the building received notice from the court. The building, through its lawyer, had failed to file a motion in time from its first submission, and so the judge ruled that the dog had been in our building for sufficient time to have him grandfathered into the constitution and ordered the building to pay costs to the dog owner. Obviously the judge owned ten dogs in the city and was always going to rule in favor of the dog.

We celebrated. The pro-dog lobby held a party, and the board held meetings to discuss how they could have failed so miserably in upholding their constitution. The dog barked loudly to say thank you, and my kids rejoiced that they could continue to play with the dog.

The board finally put out a letter and a change to the constitution that named the grandfathered dog and its right to stay, but they also put in new, really strict anti-dog laws that we all had to sign and return, which everyone did. My hopes of getting a dog were dashed further. No one but the grandfathered dog and tenant in the building could have a dog stay overnight any more. No other dogs were allowed to visit. Dogs were to be kept a safe distance from the lobby. Sight dogs were an exception, but the building needed to be informed of their presence and they couldn't stay overnight. I am surprised that the new laws didn't include a prohibition against tenants who looked like dogs or who had dog hair on their clothes or who secretly ate dog food from entering the building. What a complete fiasco. It did teach me one thing in this city: Don't mess with dog owners. They rule the world!

I now am afraid of all dog owners. I apply this fear

to my everyday contact with them. It is one of my first questions I ask anyone in Manhattan when meeting him or her for the first time. If the person answers in the affirmative, I nod and reassess my standing. I tell my kids always to ask an owner if they can pet their dogs when out in the street. First, because of the safety issue and second, because dog owners treat their dogs, in most cases, equally if not better than their own human relatives. Would you like it if a complete stranger came up to one of your kids in the street and started petting them and playing with them? Dog owners are very protective of their pets in Manhattan. If other dogs are aggressive in the street or in the numerous dog runs, confrontations start and insults get hurled commenting on the lack of discipline and respect shown by the other dog owner. Note it is never the dog's fault but always its owner. Dogs can do no wrong.

The facilities for dogs in just my neighborhood are staggering. There are at least three grooming services, all of which make so much money that they are only open for business for very limited, short periods of time. There are three pet supply stores catering mostly to dogs, where you can purchase dog food, leashes, toys, clothing, and other accessories for the canines. There are two dog runs in the park by the East River. One run is for larger dogs and one is just for smaller breeds to allow them to exercise without being run over or victimized.

On the way to the park there is a day-care center for dogs that has at least fifty dogs in it every time I pass it. I believe it turns away dogs each week because it is full. Manhattan dog owners feel extremely guilty for leaving their dogs indoors alone at home all day, so they spend vast amounts of money to ensure they have dog playdates and get the exercise they need. The day-care center is split in two, catering for larger and smaller breeds separately. For those who require slightly more intimate services for their dogs, there are dog car services that pick up and drop off to dog day-care centers in other parts of the city.

For those who will not trust centers with their dogs during the day, numerous dog walkers are spotted all over the city. Their business is a reputational one, so you hardly ever see any dog walkers being anything less than loving to the dogs they are walking. It doesn't take long for a dog owner in Manhattan to find out if any abuse has taken place.

There are four vet clinics within walking distance in our neighborhood, all of which are as expensive as seeing a human doctor and, in many cases, without any pet insurance.

No wonder we coined the phrase "It's a dog's life." I know what I would want to come back as if I were ever to believe in reincarnation, so long as it was guaranteed that I lived in Manhattan.

PART 4

Restaurants and Entertainment

CHAPTER 19

Ordering My First New York Sandwich

The fast pace of life in this city is not only reflected by the speed at which its residents and workers walk, it is evident in most activities that New Yorkers partake in every day. From the moment they wake up, commute, work, eat, and play, these city folk are constantly on the go, cramming as much as they can into their busy lives at an astonishing tempo. Nowhere is this more apparent than during lunch rush hour at a New York deli on the made-to-order sandwich and salad bar lines.

Coming from Europe, sandwiches and salads were always preprepared and stacked on shelves for hungry consumers to come along and leisurely choose which type they wanted, and then slowly walk to the cashiers and pay for it. The selection was limited to what was on display, with no substitutions and no additions. If you didn't like everything in the sandwich, then you had to remove it yourself after you paid for it. Nothing was ever freshly prepared.

Not so in New York. So long as they have

the ingredients in the store, you can have any combination of sandwich or salad that you so desire. If you want cheese, lettuce, tomato, onion, peppers, radishes, peas, carrots, lime juice, peanut butter, and watercress on a club roll with pickles, mustard, ketchup, and balsamic vinegar, they will make it for you, no problem, and charge you according to the ingredients you chose. Nothing is an issue.

The only time there is a problem is if you are undecided about what you want to order by the time you get to the front of the line.

I was a little nervous on my first day of work in a new country and a new city. I had arrived on a Sunday afternoon; the Monday after was a public holiday, and the following day was the beginning of a new chapter in my career. The first challenge of the day was to work out how to get from the Upper West Side to Midtown East by subway. As it turned out, the process was very simple and involved two stops with one change of line. I arrived thirty minutes early at the office and couldn't get onto the trading floor because no one was in. I paced around the huge lobby area, constantly looking at my watch to see when I could call up to the desk again and find out if anyone would come downstairs and put me out of my misery.

Whenever you are eager for time to move quickly the whole world seems to slow down. Seconds took minutes to complete. I was stuck in this perpetual slow motion when all around me people were whizzing past on their way to work at an astonishing speed. It felt like I was in a music video, and my mind wandered off, creating lyrics to match this perfect setting for an epic MTV-type production. In what seemed like no time at all, I had come up with the perfect song, with an incredible melody and lyrics to boot. I must have been humming quite loudly when I was tapped on the shoulder by my new boss, who had seen me pacing, singing, and waving my hands during his journey through the lobby. Not the greatest first-day impression. "Oh," he said in a rather surprised tone. "I thought you were wearing headphones." I didn't know what to say, but I could feel my mind racing away, trying to find the appropriate response but instead focusing on the thought "I can't believe he just saw me do that." My future chart-topping melody was soon long forgotten, and I shifted to correcting what seemed like my weird display in the lobby.

I was welcomed by the whole team and promptly shown to an empty desk. My computer hadn't arrived. I had no screens in front of me. The phone wasn't connected and I had nowhere to put my personal belongings. I didn't have a real desk, just a small space that was created between two other employees who had been working there for quite a while. I did have a chair, which was reassuring, and so I sat down and surveyed the new environment and what had just transpired. I had succeeded in getting to the office, albeit a little early. I had a place to sit and everyone seemed friendly at first glance. All was well.

Just when I was about to get comfortable, I was ushered away from my desk to an orientation meeting that lasted a full two hours. By the end of the presentation, I was fluent in knowing where all the emergency

exits were and who my fire marshal was. I was acquaint-
ed with the compliance, finance, human resources, and
payroll departments and had taken notes on their ex-
tension numbers. I was fingerprinted and given a new
pass to enter the building. I had signed or initialed at
least fifteen pieces of paper and had been photographed
three times. By the time I was finished, I had signed my
life away with no privacy rights still intact, and could
be fired at any minute for failure to live up to at least
one hundred stipulations that I didn't understand. I returned to my desk at noon disorientated, if not delusional, and most definitely confused.

My stomach started rumbling, and it suddenly
dawned on me that I hadn't eaten a thing yet because
of my first-day nerves. I asked the colleague to my left
what the routine was for lunch. He told me that a few
of them were going to grab a sandwich and I was more
than welcome to come along. I was ecstatic to have been
included in the lunch run on the first day, and a warm
feeling of being accepted and belonging appeared in my
belly, competing for attention with the hunger pains.

Four fairly young guys, including myself, left the
office at 12:30 p.m. with one purpose in mind: to get
a sandwich and return a few minutes later to eat at our
respective desks. One in our lunch group had a slightly
more complicated task of bringing back sandwiches for
two co-workers who remained at the office to man the
fort. I didn't even bat an eyelid at my task at hand. I had
collected a sandwich for myself on hundreds of occasions in London before, without incident.

We strolled out of the building with the conversation

focused on where I had grown up and where I now lived in Manhattan. They asked me about university and if I played any sports and if I would be interested in joining their softball league. I told them that I had never played before and everyone laughed, including me. We must have walked about two blocks west before we all turned into a huge deli-type store with several different stations inside, presenting foods from all over the world. There was a sushi bar; a Mongolian bar, which completely baffled me because a man was pouring water over a round object and moving a large wooden implement around (it didn't look that appetizing); a soup station; a salad counter where you picked the items yourself; a grill station for hot food; a station for carving huge pieces of meat that resembled a scene after a successful hunt by cavemen; and finally, the more traditional stations of sandwiches and salads where you could choose made-to-order items.

In midconversation, my small posse took its rightful place at the back of the line for the sandwich counter. There were about fifteen people in front of us. The line snaked off slightly toward the made-to-order salad section that was very noisy and active with bowls, vegetables, and pincer-like objects flying around at an extraordinary pace. The dialogue at the sandwich line had moved on to how I was coping with Manhattan life, and I was rather enjoying being center stage among new and interested colleagues. The line was moving quite swiftly along, and I wasn't really paying much attention to the etiquette of ordering ahead of me. I had my back to the counter where orders were placed and continued chatting nonchalantly until, from behind me, I heard one of my colleagues rapidly call out his sandwich order for himself and the two other colleagues back at the office.

I couldn't believe my ears. In the time it takes Usain Bolt to run a hundred-meter dash, my co-worker had given instructions for three completely different yet remarkably similar sandwiches to a deli employee who spoke pidgin English at best, and the whole monologue had been understood word for word. The sandwiches were assembled in equally astonishing time, scooped up by the customer, and being paid for at the check-out counter some five feet away. The actual sandwich order was:

"Can I please have three BLT sandwiches, one with extra lettuce—make that shredded, not whole lettuce—two with mayo, not the one with extra lettuce, and the dry one with a slice of light Swiss cheese. Oh, and the extra lettuce should be on a toasted club roll and for the other two: one on whole wheat and one on seven grain. Thanks."

Presto! It was done. And then it dawned on me. It was my turn.

My eyes and ears were still on the person who had just placed this insane order, and I inadvertently didn't hear the command " Next!" Apparently, the server had asked me for my order with the cunning use of the word "next" three times, and in the sandwich world, it's three strikes and you are out. It was somebody else's turn now. My other colleagues were placing their contrived sandwich orders, and refused to make any eye contact with me as I was left stranded in sandwich limbo at the front of the counter with no order having been placed and no one paying me the slightest bit of attention. Sandwich purgatory!

I muscled up enough courage to attract one of the employees' attention with a loud, "Excuse me, I would like to place a sandwich order if I may, please." I could not have sounded any more British, and as soon as I said it I wanted to disappear. Everyone behind me started laughing, making fun of my accent. For a few split seconds, the enormous tension at the sandwich bar had been broken at my expense and comic relief had shone through. I still hadn't placed the order, and when the laughing stopped the impatient masses behind me began calling out abusive adjectives to describe my indecision. A Manhattan lunch sandwich seeker, on limited time, is extremely creative in hurling insults at the weaker, less experienced foreign novice. The best line I heard that day was, "You at the front, if you order a snail sandwich, I'll call the cops on you for cannibalism."

The truth was, I had no idea in my mind what sandwich I wanted. The sandwich maker, who had just two minutes ago understood every word of the most complicated lunch order ever made, suddenly only conversed in Spanish. This left me no longer hungry and in a somewhat dazed-and-confused state. I rejoined my group void of any sandwich, and picked up a squashed corn muffin in a plastic wrapper that was near the checkout counter as a rather poor, unappetizing substitute. After all, I had to leave the deli with something to avoid being the subject of derision for the rest of the day. I

paid for it quickly, deposited the few nickels and cop-
pers of change into the tip bowl, and exited the premises sharply. I was shell-shocked. I had been stampeded
by a herd of hungry New Yorkers.

My colleagues tried explaining to me on the short
walk back to work that this would happen to me every
day unless I knew exactly what I wanted before I entered any rush-hour lunch establishment in Manhattan.
This incident had propelled the subject of fast food into
a modern, supersonic New York category.

It was two months before I mustered up enough
resolve to retry the process, and in the meantime, relied
on others to get my lunch when they went out and bring
it back to me at my desk. How I longed for the ready-
made sandwich shops in London where you could gaze
into the glass displays for hours until you finally made
up your mind.

CHAPTER 20

Restaurants and Reservations

There are over eighteen thousand eating establishments in the five boroughs of New York. There are no specific numbers for Manhattan, but considering it is the entertainment capital of New York City, if not the world, then the numbers probably run into the several thousand. You can have breakfast, lunch, and dinner at a different eating establishment each and every day in Manhattan for a few years before you start repeating. No other city in the world offers its consuming inhabitants the sheer number of choices and unbelievable variety of cuisine that Manhattan does. This is culinary paradise.

This Garden of Eating is a huge magnet for attracting visitors from all over the world. Restaurants from every inhabited continent blossom here and compete for business from an ever-exploratory-minded customer base. You can eat in an underground cave as well as on top of a soaring skyscraper. You can eat in private rooms or on communal tables. You can eat at chef's tables in the kitchen or outside on the street, weather permitting.

You can devour the finest ingredients served on the best china using expensive sterling silver as utensils, or eat with your hands at establishments where, by custom, any silverware is frowned upon. In Manhattan, many restaurants are open all night and are crowded even in the wee hours. Spoiled for choice, many residents of Manhattan take full advantage of this smorgasbord of restaurants, providing they can afford to eat out on a regular basis. With a never-ending source of eateries to consume in or get meals delivered to your home from, it is no wonder that many apartment kitchens in New York City remain underutilized.

Chefs from all over the world flock to Manhattan to try to open restaurants bearing their name. Faced with stiff competition, many don't succeed. Established eateries can fall by the wayside because when relatively inexpensive long-term leases expire, many restaurateurs are put off renewal by extortionate rent increases. Manhattan can either be a gold mine for those who have the much-needed combination of cooking ability, a niche product, a fabulous location, and good business acumen, or a graveyard for many who lack one or more of the attributes listed above. Even with this high turnover of restaurants, many thrive year after year, filling their tables with loyal clientele enjoying gloriously prepared dishes from all over the globe.

New, trendy restaurants appealing to savvy Manhattan residents and visitors with high disposable incomes open their doors for the first time each month. Millions of dollars are spent on the décor and ambiance inside, while outside, public relations officers and marketers get to work on selling the stylishness and hype factors of the restaurant to the "in crowd." Opening nights are glamorous affairs, with paparazzi blinding the lucky few invitees with their flash photography as the trendsetters make their entrances. Newspapers write mouth-watering reviews in their eating-out sections, and blogs and Web sites are abuzz with hits and comments about how wonderful these new restaurants are. The success of these establishments obviously depends on the quality of the food first and foremost, but also on how long they can maintain their hipness. If the elite are not talking about them or frequenting them, then they can fall out of favor pretty rapidly. With the wrong ingredients in place (and I am not talking about what is on the plate), the somewhat fickle New Yorker foodie can determine which way the pendulum inevitably swings between success and failure.

My wife and I often go out to dinner with another couple. Whenever my wife informs me of an up-and-coming arrangement with this couple there is one thing I know for certain: we will be eating at a new, hip establishment where we have never eaten before. The first few times we did this were extremely exciting. The whole evening was like perpetually sitting on the edge of your seat, waiting for the food to arrive to see if it lived up to its reputation. The whole experience felt like an adventure, as if we had all turned into food critics and our opinions greatly mattered to the success of the restaurant. I felt privileged to be one of the early few to devour new eclectic dishes and survey the ambiance of a beautifully renovated space.

However, after partaking in a few of these evenings, I finally realized that being a food guinea pig was somewhat dull. I liked eating at restaurants where I knew the food was good because I had eaten there before, and where I understood the menu and didn't feel the need to be a participant in a gastronomic survey. What amused me even more was the reason the other couple liked to try out new places. After every meal, I would ask them what they thought of the food and the restaurant. Their response first focused on the food and this varied in scale, from "Spectacular" to "Uninspiring" to "We will never come back here again." These food critics would always end with the line, "At least we can tell people that we have eaten here," thus proving that with new Manhattan eateries, it is as much about the hype as it is about the food.

In my numerous years of eating here, I have had the fortune of being wined and dined at some of New York's finest restaurants, mainly due to business meals where I am the customer (and therefore do not have to foot the bill). These select few restaurants receive extremely high ratings from the many New York City guidebooks. I have been knocked off my feet by some of them with their exemplary standards of cuisine, service, and décor, and have been outraged by others for their sheer snootiness and disregard for the customer.

An evening of fine dining in Manhattan is usually a memorable event and a positive experience. To be pampered at a top-class restaurant costs a fortune, and in return for parting with hard-earned dollars, one expects exceptional quality of food and top-class service to accompany it. In the vast majority of cases, this has been my experience. Although, one glaring exception comes to mind....

I was invited out to dinner by a group of vendors who were celebrating the end of their financial year by entertaining their top customers at a restaurant of our choosing here in Manhattan. I was the fortunate one who was asked to pick the venue, and I chose one I had never eaten at before but had only heard good things about. This was a place where I would have eaten only on a very special occasion, as the cost was one of the highest in the city. I was very excited about the evening because I particularly enjoyed the people who would be joining me. One of the perks of living in the city is that if you have a business dinner in Manhattan, it is possible to return home after work, spend some quality time with the family, help put young ones to bed, and still go out into the night and be on time to any business function. I was refreshed from the short stay at home and rejuvenated at being able to combine business and pleasure with the small window of time afforded me by my busy schedule. I donned my best suit and favorite tie for the occasion and headed out, relishing the prospect of what was in store for me.

Arriving at the restaurant on time, I was greeted by the five associates who had not had the fortune of being able to go home first, because they lived in the suburbs. They had all worked later than usual, and then had a couple of cocktails to get the evening started before they met up with me. My coat was duly taken and whisked away by a valet in exchange for a numbered ticket, and we were promptly ushered to our table by a very friendly and efficient maitre d'. We were seated at a circular table, and I quickly noticed the wonderful Wedgwood china plates and beautiful crystal glasses immaculately positioned on the fine linens that covered the table. The chairs were immensely comfortable. All in all, the first impressions were very favorable. I immediately began to relax.

I ordered a cocktail to start my evening off, settling on a scotch on the rocks, which was brought to me in a timely fashion. With the first sip I felt a warn tingly sensation and thought for a moment about how lucky I was to be at a top-class dining establishment in Manhattan, celebrating another successful year with very decent business associates for whom I had the utmost respect. I ate a little bread, sipped some more of the cocktail, and engaged in festive conversation about the up-and-coming holidays. Menus were handed out and the dialogue came to a sudden halt as we started reading about delectable appetizers and mouth-watering entrees. My eyes immediately honed in on my favorite fish in the world and one not too easily found in New York: the Dover sole, who swims mostly in European waters and is considered a delicacy. I didn't want anything heavy for the first course and decided on a salad with four types of lettuce, a poached pear, beets, and a drizzle of some type of citrus fruit. The waiter took all the orders. Most of the others ordered shellfish of some variety, with the exception of one who only ever ate meat, so he ordered their finest steak with all the usual accompaniments.

At this juncture I politely asked to be excused, wiped my mouth with my napkin so as to dislodge any remnants of bread crumbs that may have formed at the corners of my mouth, and went to the washroom. It was immaculate. The toilet seats had been shined to a polish, and the sinks and countertops were spotless. The soap dispenser that stood next to the sink particularly enamored me. I picked it up to take a closer look, as it was strikingly handsome, and was gently caressing it when another customer entered. I put the dispenser down and walked toward the exit, followed by the eyes of the other customer who was, not surprisingly, giving me strange looks. I returned to the table and sat down as a waiter loitered over me, ready to redeposit my napkin on my lap, as is traditional at fine dining establishments.

A few minutes later, three waiters arrived at the table armed with appetizers and in sync placed them in front of us. In turn, the headwaiter of this group, with the finest of French accents, slowly explained each dish in tremendous detail, his descriptions interspersed with French words describing the dishes as if they were works of art on display for all to see. The food was so well presented it seemed a shame to eat it. My salad was an explosion of color, from the redness of the beets to the greens of the leaves, all arranged in glorious patterns that fanned the plate. The tastes of each dish matched the visual effects, and moans of delight oozed out of everyone's mouth as orgasmic morsels of flavor bombarded our pallets.

The plates were cleared in an orderly fashion, and everyone discussed how fantastic the starters had been.

I couldn't wait for my Dover sole. I hadn't eaten one since I had left England, and had begun to think that I would have to wait until I went back to London on a business trip to fulfill my desires, until I saw it on this menu. The sole was to be plain, grilled, and served with some fingerling potatoes and a selection of seasonal vegetables tied up in a parcel. We waited for about five minutes, making toasts for the holidays and paying each other a whole host of compliments about achievements that had taken place throughout the year. Waiter activity began to pick up around our section of the room as a preparation table was wheeled out next to us. From out of nowhere, three waiters, holding two plates covered in a silver top with a handle, positioned themselves around the table and placed the plates at each serving place. With each waiter poised with his hands on two different tops, the lead waiter counted to three, and in unison the six lids were removed, revealing the most amazing display of gorgeously arranged food on five of the plates. Everyone gasped in sheer delight at what he saw before him.

I looked at my plate. It was empty. I looked at my waiter and down again at my plate and then back at him. My two neighbors glanced toward my plate also. I picked it up, looked underneath it, and made a sarcastic comment that maybe my Dover sole was hiding somewhere. Within an instant, the maitre d' was standing over me. He bent forward and whispered in my ear.

"I am so sorry, but we appear to be out of Dover sole. Can I get you something else?"

Nobody else moved. I was the customer with five

salesmen from the same company whose sole purpose that night was to thank me for my business with a fantastic meal; the end result was my plate was void of food. The host of our soiree started to speak to the maitre d', but I promptly waved him off and said I would handle this. I told everyone else to start as the food would get cold, but no one reached for his utensils. I said, "I won't address this issue until everyone starts to eat," which they fittingly did.

"What happened to my sole?" I asked, feeling like a kid who had been let down in receiving a present that had been promised.

"We have run out and didn't realize it until we had plated all the other entrees. So what can I get you instead, sir?" the maitre d' said. He offered suggestions and clutched a menu to his chest.

"I will tell you what I want," I replied rather harshly. "I would love a Dover sole."

I turned away from him and started a conversation with the gentleman to my left, leaving the maitre d' leaning over me with his mouth wide open, speechless. He cleared his throat and, yet again, replied that he had no Dover sole to offer me.

"What would you like instead? A nice piece of cod or haddock or maybe halibut, prepared in any way you wish, sir?" He was looking rather pleased with his suggestions for alternatives, sure that I would pick one of them and the matter would be finished and we could all move on.

"I'll tell you what I would like instead," I said, raising my voice so that other tables nearby would be alerted to the scandal taking place at ours. "Instead, I would like a ... Dover sole, please." I finished my sentence and kept my head still fixated on the face of the maitre d', awaiting his response. I was purposely being provocative and arrogant. I didn't want anything else. The spoilt child that has a tendency to rear its ugly head inside all of us was hard at work that night for me. I told him to call up another restaurant and get a Dover sole delivered here.

Everyone at the table urged me to order something else, with many offering half of their meals, which was very nice. But I was adamant in my refusal. It was Dover sole versus nothing for me. And nothing won.

The maitre d' and the rest of the staff left our table shaking their heads, looking like diplomats who had just had an olive branch rejected by a feuding opponent in negotiations. So I sat there telling my hosts not to worry and to enjoy their meals. This was the biggest conversation stopper and made everyone at the table feel extremely uncomfortable.

In hindsight, I should have ordered something else and let it go, but I was angry that I had been put in this situation. Restaurants run out of choices and specials every night but inform their customers before everyone else is served. I just thought it was wrong.

A few minutes later, the maitre d' returned to the table and asked me if there was anything he could get me as a token of his regret for this most unfortunate incident. It suddenly dawned on me. There was an item that I wanted. I said, "Yes, actually there is something you can give me. I would love to take home your soap dispenser from the bathroom. I think it is stunning."

He staggered back away from the table looking perplexed at the outrageousness of my request. He stood there motionless for a while, trying to ascertain whether I was being serious or not, and then he smiled. "Certainly, sir, I will get it wrapped for you this instant and place it in a bag," he said, realizing that if this made the customer happy and got me off his back, then so be it. This cheap but ornate item could obviously be replaced the next day, and a few bars of soap in a dish would suffice for the rest of the night.

I'm not relaying this story so you can visit any Manhattan restaurant and if something goes wrong choose items of art from the walls to take home with you. It was simply my reaction to this particular situation and I took advantage of it. I went home hungry, not so angry anymore but happy that I was armed with a new soap dispenser. We still have it, while I have a reputation of being a little stubborn and a bit quirkier than previously thought.

Reservations

Most restaurants have Web sites that display menus and allow the customer to order takeout or delivery online. There are restaurants whose Web sites ingeniously allow the customer to make reservations electronically. Many exclusive restaurants remove themselves from this method just to be aloof, or only advertise available dining times that many find impossible to utilize as they are either too early in the evening or too late at night. I prefer to make reservations online for the number of neighborhood restaurants that I frequent. Any system that can take out people from the process is less likely to mess up. Humans forget to write down the name properly or the correct number of people in the party and get confused over times.

Most restaurants in Manhattan take reservations one month in advance. Some use a thirty-day system, and others who like to have their tables reserved well in advance will stretch the process out to two months. Every day at 9:00 a.m., the phones ring off the hook at the most popular of eateries, taking reservations for a day that has just become free sometime in the future. The most sought-after times in Manhattan are between 7:00 p.m. and 9:00 p.m., and these book up the earliest.

My wife often makes me call restaurants that are impossible to get into a few days before I want a reservation. I normally am asking for a Thursday or Saturday night at around 8:00 p.m. for four people. Usually when I speak to the reservationist, I start the phone call off very politely: "I know I am asking the impossible, but do you happen to have a table for four this Thursday at 8:00 p.m.?" The responses vary. I never hear "Certainly sir, may I take your name?" I either have to listen to a pack of hyenas laughing down the line in response to my delusional request, or I get offered a table for afternoon tea or a midnight snack, which I decline. I then get into an argument with my wife over why she always makes me do this and how many times do I have to face rejection? She then informs me that I have to do as I am told, and that the probability of me getting a successful last-minute booking at a fabulous Manhattan restaurant is increasing because of the number of rejections I have amassed.

Last month, I had to again put myself through the rigors of reservation turndown because my wife screamed out from the shower, "Please see if our favorite Italian can take us tonight at eight for four. I forgot to make a reservation." When I got off the phone I went into the bathroom to speak to her. When she saw me smiling at her she asked, "Well, did we get in?" I answered, "Yes, a table at eight for four was no problem." She retorted, "Told you it work one day," looking ever so proud of herself in having proved me wrong.

I quickly added, in a sarcastic tone, "Of course, they don't have a table at that time for tonight. I was kidding!" I luckily ducked as a bar of soap went whizzing past where my head was mere seconds before. I wasn't so lucky with the shower sponge as I was still in the crouch position and presented a somewhat large target to hit. My humor doesn't seem to go down too well an hour before dinner with nowhere to go.

There are numerous private concierges for the Manhattan elite who need "ins" at all the right places. I once used one of these when I was desperate for a reservation for a business colleague who had asked for one particular booking at a hard-to-get-into spot, giving me six weeks to get my act together before he flew in from overseas. I, of course, completely forgot until he reminded me two days before he was to arrive that we were meeting there at eight for dinner, along with two other people he was bringing. I had no reservation. I had never placed the call. I called the restaurant hastily and was dealt with by a waiter or maitre d' who had a PhD in how to be condescending to customers who call up late for a booking. The conversation was very short and very predictable.

I called up the concierge service, and before I even introduced myself I had already pleaded, begged, and promised to give the woman who answered the phone my whole inheritance if she could get me into this downtown Italian in two nights' time at eight o'clock for four people. She first laughed, which I took as an awful sign. Was she one of those hyenas too? She explained that the cost was $75 for the booking, it would be charged to my American Express account, and that she was laughing at the thought of someone giving up his inheritance for a single reservation booking because it would probably cost me less to buy the restaurant. She said she would have to call back in an hour. I was on edge for the next sixty minutes and expected the worst. She had warned me that she wasn't always successful and that this particular restaurant gave her a hard time, but she would do her best.

One hour and six minutes later (and I know that because I was watching the clock), she called back. I answered with a quiet hello and closed my eyes, expecting the bad news and the end of a prosperous relationship with my overseas co-worker. She asked if this was I, and with an affirmative reply, she immediately informed me of her success. I was flabbergasted. I couldn't help myself in asking her how the heck she managed to get in. She wouldn't say how she had succeeded, and to this day I have no idea how Manhattan concierges do their job. The most likely answer is that the top, trendy restaurants in Manhattan always keep a few tables back in case a celebrity or a media person wants a last-minute dinner, and that backhander payments thrive in a whole web of underworld restaurant reservation mob-type behavior. We had the meal two nights later. Unfortunately, it was dreadful, and my colleague who insisted on eating there swore he would never come back. Go figure!

It was my wife's birthday on October 20. I asked her where she wanted to celebrate. She came up with the name of an expensive restaurant. It was just under two months before her birthday. I didn't sweat. I put an electronic reminder into my cell phone to call one month before. I was prepared. At 9:01 a.m. thirty-one days before her actual birthday, I called up the restaurant to book a table. This is what transpired:

"Hello, can I help you?"

"Is this such-and-such restaurant?"

"Yes, it is. Can I help you? One second, sir, can I put you on hold?"

"Yes, you can."

"Thank you."

Brazilian samba music played on the telephone as I waited and my head bobbed up and down to the beat.

"Sorry to keep you waiting, sir. How can I help you?"

"I would like to make a reservation, please."

"What date, please, sir?"

"October 20, please."

"How many people in your party, please?"

"Two."

"Last name?"

"Silverman."

"What time, please?"

"Anytime between 7:00 p.m. and 9:00 p.m. I am not fussed, to tell you the truth."

This was all going rather well, I thought. My wife would be happy that I remembered to make a reservation, and I would be happy because she was happy.

The reservationist paused for a few seconds and then said, "OK, thank you for all that information, sir. The next available table we have for the two of you is November 18 at 5:30 p.m. Shall I make that reservation for you now, sir?"

I was stunned into silence.

"Hello, sir, are you still there?"

"Why on earth did you ask me the time and the number of people for October 20? Why did you make me go through the whole process if you knew it wasn't available?"

"Mr. Silverman, do you want the reservation on November 18 at 5:30 p.m. or not, as I have three people waiting on the phone?" she said in a rather nasty tone.

I was furious and wanted to scream obscenities at her. Instead, out of my mouth came, "I will never eat at your restaurant for the rest of my life. I don't care if you are the last restaur—" Click. The phone went dead. I had been rejected, teased, tormented, and then disconnected. Bravo to New York restaurants and to the complete arrogance of some of them in the way they treat people. I still have never eaten there. I hear it's fabulous. I have told numerous people my story in hopes that someone would join my boycott. Even my wife has eaten there, just not on her birthday and not with me. And they are still sold out every night.

And I hadn't done my research. They take advance bookings for sixty days, not thirty.

CHAPTER 21

Manhattan Movie Etiquette

The first time I ever went to the movies in Manhattan was back in 1985, when I went to see Rocky IV at a movie theatre near Times Square. The movie was released during the heart of the cold war when Ronald Reagan was president. I went to the movie with a blind date that had been set up by my cousin. We met outside the theatre, and I purchased the tickets, some popcorn, and a couple of sodas. It was in the middle of the day during the workweek, but even so, the place was packed. We had arrived a good twenty minutes before the movie started but still found it hard to get good viewing seats that were together. We ended up sitting about ten rows from the front against the far wall.

The first thing that I observed about the movie theatre was that it was so noisy. In Europe when you go to a movie you sit down and wait quietly for the program to start. Here, everyone was talking, hardly anyone was actually in his or her seat, and large groups were attending the movie together. The second thing I noticed was that my date wasn't the slightest bit interested in me. I tried polite conversation and was dismayed at the one-word answers that made up her responses. She hadn't asked me a single question in the short time we had known each other. I was looking forward to the movie since the early dinner that we were supposed to have afterward was going to be torturous and exhausting with me doing all the talking.

The commercials began, followed by the previews. It was quiet, apart from the annoying munching and ruffling sounds that accompany movies in the United States because of the obsession with popcorn. It was apparent that most of the moviegoers present had some type of superstition that they couldn't begin eating popcorn until the movie started. I had virtually finished my box when it dawned on me that my date hadn't eaten a single kernel. When the lights went down and the projector started working overtime, my date went to town on her popcorn with rapid hand-to-mouth motions that I could see out of the corner of my left eye. This continuous pattern of hand in box, rustling noise, hand to mouth, munching noise continued for thirty minutes. The only pause in this routine was an occasional slurp of the soda through a straw, but she had positioned the cup in a holder on the seat armrest that enabled her to keep her hand in the popcorn box at the same time. I actually found watching her more interesting than the previews, but an awkward situation arose when she turned her head toward me and our eyes met for the first time: she gave me a stare that sent the message "Stop looking at me, freak."

For those of you who stopped watching Rocky movies after the first one, Rocky IV is an excuse for Russian bashing and highlighting good old America versus the Evil Empire. I realized this as soon as the movie started and was dreading the next ninety minutes of propaganda, Hollywood-style. What I didn't expect was that the vast majority of the audience would treat the movie as if it were a live broadcast of a boxing match between two archenemies, and that the audience would act as if they could directly affect the outcome of the bout. During the boxing scenes, moviegoers would get out of their seats cheering, clapping, and shouting abuse at the Russian boxer. I thought a riot was going to take place.

I had little choice but to join in.

I was high-fived by the person sitting next to me, and together we started a chant of "Rocky, Rocky" that echoed around the auditorium. I had never experienced anything like it. Everyone but my date was standing up clapping, waving arms, and shouting encouragement to Rocky. Finally my date stood up; I was happy to see that she wasn't a living corpse. She moved closer to me, and right in the middle of the heat of battle, she said, "I'm leaving. Thanks. Bye."

And off she went, walking down the row of seats, muttering "Excuse me" to everyone, and then pushed open the door at the back of the theatre and was gone. For a split second I thought that she obviously didn't like the movie, but then appreciated that she liked me less than the movie and that my chanting with the rest of the crowd hadn't helped my cause too much either.

I shrugged my shoulders and carried on watching, getting ever more involved in the mayhem that erupted with Rocky's heroic win against all the odds. The crowd in the movie theatre went berserk, and when the credits rolled and the lights came up, all cheered and chanted Rocky's name as we left the building and found ourselves in daylight back out on the street. I looked around to try to find the person who had high-fived me to talk about the movie but couldn't see anyone I knew. The movie crowd had blended into the mass of pedestrians, and I walked toward the subway thinking about how this was an amazing New York experience and far more exciting than watching the same movie back in London. The whole afternoon had cost me about $15, and I was spared the annoyance of dinner with someone who couldn't stand the sight of me.

Twenty-five years later, I have movie date nights with my wife. We walk to the movie theatre with our tickets already purchased, and the whole evening now costs $150. The breakdown of the cost is as follows. Two tickets to the movie, including processing fee for ordering online: $30. Two bags of popcorn; two waters; a pack of some squidgy, gummy substance; and a pack of some chocolate-covered something: $50. Four hours of babysitting: $70. Throw in a dinner and a drink afterward at a neighborhood restaurant, and the cost of the evening out spirals out of control.

We love going to the movies in Manhattan. The cold war has since ended, and scenes like I saw in Times Square are now a rarity. Occasionally, the audience breaks out into spontaneous applause at the end of a

thrilling movie, and during horror scenes many specta-
tors scream in shock at the scenes developing on-screen.
Going to the movies is a major form of escape, and we
both like to see shows that enrich our lives and that we
can discuss afterward over dinner or back at home. Unfortunately, my wife can testify that I am one of the biggest emotional wrecks in most dramatic movies I watch.
In the original Rocky, I cry every time I see the scene
where Rocky is running up the stairs in Philadelphia
followed by a whole crowd. I bawl my eyes out during Chariots of Fire when Harold Abrahams wins the
one-hundred-meter sprint final at the Paris Olympics of
1924. My worst performance is during the French toast
scene during Kramer vs. Kramer, in which I sob uncon-
trollably on seeing the plight of a divorced father and
child. At the end of the vast majority of the films we see
together, we stay behind in our seats as the credits are
running, not to see who the gaffer or grip holders are,
but to wait until I have finished wiping my eyes and the
redness and puffiness from crying has started to fade.

Most moviegoers in Manhattan have a set routine about what time they need to arrive at the theatre,
where they sit in the auditorium, what they eat and
drink, and what quirks are permitted during the showing of the movie. My wife and I are no exception. Our
routine is very specific to our needs. We spend a lot of
time during the week discussing which movie we want
to watch on the weekend. We used to take turns to
choose, but I had to forfeit three years' worth of choices for making my wife watch five consecutive British
gangster films, in which the lack of subtitles prevented

her from understanding the dialogue and much of the plot. As a subtle form of retribution, I was forced to sit through a whole series of movies where I could count on one hand the number of men in attendance.

Once we have agreed on which movie we are going to see, we then survey the times that best suit our busy schedule. The one rule is that my wife has to put the baby to bed, and then the rest of the evening is free. If the movie has a published start time of 7:00 p.m., the movie will not begin until at least 7:20 p.m., taking into account advertisements and previews. We therefore buy separate tickets online using different credit cards. We either print off the tickets at home or use the machines in the lobby at the theatre. I leave the apartment at 6:15 p.m. and walk the five minutes to the movie theatre. I present my single ticket to the usher and buy the popcorn, candy, and drinks. I then sit in the same seat no matter which theatre it is. (When you enter the cinema facing the screen, always walk to the far side and start walking down the farthest aisle. Thirteen rows down, take the seats in the middle section that are closest to the passageway.) I sit in the aisle seat and reserve the seat next to me for my wife. I then take out a crossword puzzle, munch on some popcorn, and savor a rare moment of solitude.

I'll watch as the rest of the moviegoers file in. Those like me who get to the theatre early enough sit in a preferred viewing spot. The closer to the preannounced movie time, the more frustrated the paying customer becomes. Arguments break out between married couples as one blames the other for tardiness as they struggle to find any decent seats together. The first three rows are always the last to be filled as watching a movie from this vantage point is a precursor for admittance into the hospital that same night with chronic neck pains. Hoards of latecomers patrol the gangways looking for empty seats. I get asked several times if the vacant seat next to me is taken. Apparently my coat, a box of popcorn, and a drink lying on the seat are not enough visual evidence that the seat has been reserved. On one occasion, a nice middle-aged lady informed me close to movie time that my date had stood me up and that I seemed like a decent enough person for her to be my date for the evening. Were she twenty years younger and I weren't married and my wife weren't en route, I may have considered it.

Much to the annoyance of the still-displaced wandering moviegoer, my wife strolls in with her single ticket exactly as the adverts finish and the previews start. Those who have loitered near me in hopes that a no-show was on the agenda file away disappointed, and my wife takes her seat, puts her candy and popcorn and drink on her lap, and immediately starts to unwind. Mission accomplished. We talk about the previews as they appear on-screen and give thumbs up or down as to whether we would want to see films that will be playing sometime in the future.

As soon as the main feature starts, we stop all conversation and follow exact movie theatre etiquette, placing cellphones on vibrate and keeping as still as possible. We have also developed a really good facial expression and sudden head movement toward others if they start talking during the movie. We do this in unison to have double the effect. Most take note immediately, but others need a polite, small verbal reminder of "quiet or go home if you want to talk." When the paid entertainment has finished and I am dry-eyed, we take our time in strolling home, timing our entrance with a round monetary number for the babysitting fee we have to pay. Going to the movies is one of our best evenings out, but for those who don't have a set routine, it can be a very frustrating and annoying experience.

CHAPTER 22

Shops and Shopping

Ask anyone from abroad for the primary non-business reason for coming to Manhattan, and in the vast majority of cases they will say shopping. This applies to both men and women, who state that New York City offers the best variety and value second to none worldwide.

Unlike in most other major metropolises, there isn't one distinct shopping area. Fifth Avenue between Fifty-ninth Street and Thirty-second Street is renowned for its high-end department and famous brand-name stores. Soho now boasts many of the world's top designers and has really rivaled Madison Avenue from Ninety-sixth Street to Forty-second Street for chic boutiques and famous named stores. In Greenwich Village, on Third Avenue on the Upper East Side, and on Columbus Avenue on the Upper West Side, you still find small, fashionable family-run shops. Whereas ten years ago Manhattan was void of the national chain stores that paraded themselves in suburbia, they have popped up in abundance, turning the exclusivity of Manhattan stores into a myth these days.

High rents and unforgiving landlords, together with a need from huge chains to be seen in Manhattan, have driven the local store owners out of business. Some of these stores had been around for generations, and it's a sad occurrence these days that whenever a store closes, a huge bank or large drugstore moves in. There also seems to be a coffee store from Seattle on every corner too, making traditionalists very upset with the direction that New York City shop-front space is heading. It doesn't look likely that this trend will ever be reversed, as recently Manhattan welcomed the final nail in the coffin: a Costco, complete with parking for which it has the audacity to charge for.

Up until thirty years ago, the huge department stores used to be exclusively in Manhattan. When they needed to expand revenues, the logical step was to open branches all over the United States. The strategists for these stores did, however, maintain that the Manhattan headquarters would also be their flagship stores. Therefore, even if one of these department stores is located in a suburban mall, outsiders still make the trip in to shop at the original, where shelves are better stocked and prices can be more competitive.

The thrill of shopping in New York City has never gone away. There is still something magical about walking down Fifth Avenue and popping in and out of its famous stores without having to drive to the mall.

Many New Yorkers have personal shoppers at

various locations in the city. I always accompany my wife on shopping trips to the department stores, and therefore I am her personal shopper. I am extremely honest in shaking my head or nodding my approval at every dress, skirt, shirt, and sweater that are thrust in my direction for help in making a purchasing decision. I think my mere presence reduces the amount spent in one spree, as when a budget that I have set in my mind is met, my attitude changes abruptly: I quickly announce that time is up and that we need to leave. My wife thinks it is because she has exhausted my patience, but the real reason is a wish not to remortgage our apartment so she can have an expensive pair of shoes.

I thought that these trips with me were the only shopping excursions that my wife took, but I soon realized that most of the assistants in the stores knew my wife by name. However, my wife does value my opinion, and for the most part I enjoy accompanying her. It is also a fantastic people-watching exercise. How else could I hang out in women's apparel sections without arousing suspicion?

I do have a personal shopper at one store. I hate shopping for myself and refuse to take my wife with me when I need to buy clothes. We always get into an argument at the store when I have to buy something one size bigger than the previous year. Twice a year, once for summer and once for winter, I walk into a huge department store in Manhattan, go find the woman I use, and tell her exactly what I am looking for. In a matter of a couple of hours, I have bought an entire wardrobe for a reasonable price, and have it all delivered to my apartment by the time I have left the store, had some lunch, and walked home.

New York women are experts in overbuying. If they need a dress for a party that is on the horizon, they will purchase three of them for comparison, wear one, and take back the other two. The indecision on what to wear is simply astonishing. Women all over this city open up their closets, staring at hundreds of their items of clothing, and announce to their partners that they have absolutely nothing to wear.

A few days before the event we have been invited to, I am asked to stop what I am doing and come into the bedroom for a fashion show. It is imperative that I have an opinion and that I choose the same dress that my wife has intended on wearing. It is a very simple exercise: Watch for facial expressions, hair movements, and body language. If you guess right, the process stops immediately as she has had a second opinion verify what she had already determined previously. If you guess wrong, initially a minicrisis ensues, causing chaos and disaster and threats of staying home and boycotting the event. It is no use correcting yourself once you have guessed wrong as this only further complicates matters. Dress rehearsals are very delicate matters and getting it right the first time prevents trips to other stores that may be even more expensive and then a repeat home fashion show.

CHAPTER 23

A Manhattan Calendar Year

New York City is the parade capital of the world. Every ethnic group seems to hold an annual one. The most famous are the Puerto Rican Day parade, Columbus Day parade, the Salute to Israel parade, the Macy's Thanksgiving Day parade, Veterans Day parade, and St. Patrick's Day parade. I can't mention parades without including the infamous Norwegian-American 17 May parade and the Korean Harvest Day parade in October.

For a full list of every parade in New York City go to:www.carnaval.com/cityguides/newyork/parades.htm. This Web site informs the knowledge-hungry parade seeker of the dates, times, and locations of every procession in each calendar year in New York City. All of these parades are tremendous spectacles for the whole family to enjoy and introduce New Yorkers to different cultures that make up the fabric of the city. There are normally marching bands, elaborate costumes, and exotic floats to listen to and set eyes upon, and the colors and smells of delicious foods line the streets as the carnivals crawl slowly up or down their designated routes.

My advice is to keep a copy of the parade schedule handy. On any given Sunday, one of my kids attends a birthday party on the Upper West Side across town, where a vast majority of their friends live. At about two o'clock in the afternoon, my wife will yell something across the apartment about one of the kids having to be at Seventy-ninth and Broadway for a gym party and that I need to take her there, hang out somewhere for ninety minutes, and then bring her home. I leave the apartment, allowing thirty minutes travel time by car to arrive on time. Armed only with one child and a birthday present for the person throwing the party, I call down to the doorman to inform him that we need the garage door opened to let our car out.

After buckling my child and myself into the car, I turn onto Second Avenue, head south for one block, and then turn right onto Seventy-ninth Street to cross the park between Fifth Avenue and Central Park West.

Unfortunately, most parents schedule children's parties in cahoots with the City Parade Planning Committee, since when I get to Seventy-ninth and Madison Avenue I am notified by a uniformed police officer, manning a barricade, that it is not possible to cross the park at this juncture. I ask him why and he tells me that seventy-five thousand Greek nationals are celebrating Greek Independence Day with a march on Fifth Avenue. I then have to head north, search for an open park crossing, and eventually arrive at 116th Street. I cross the park and have to sit in traffic on the Upper West

Side for thirty-seven blocks to get my child to the party. On days like this, we arrive forty-five minutes late, just in time for cake. I have to double-park to bring my kid to the event and get dirty looks from the parents who are throwing it. I look at them and say, "Greek parade. Who knew?" They obviously have no clue what I am talking about and usher my child into the party, turning their backs on me.

I return to my car and find a parking ticket pasted to the windshield with its corners flapping against the wipers, and open it to see a whopping $85 fine payable in the next ten days. I then drive around for the remainder of the party looking for a nonexistent parking space and end up sticking it in a lot for $20. I call my wife to tell her that all of the children are banned from birthday parties until they are old enough to catch a bus there and back by themselves. If I were organized enough to know when each parade took place, I could then make arrangements to leave the day before and stay in a hotel across town with the invited child and thus guarantee to get him or her to the party on time.

There is something for everyone in New York City. Aside from the parades, the city is crammed full of museums, art exhibitions, concert venues, sports teams, community centers, and theatres. Each month has something going on that represents a unique New York City experience. In January there is the ball drop in Times Square to usher in the New Year. February brings along the Westminster Kennel Club dog show. Beware the ides of March, as just after it comes St. Patrick's Day mayhem. April means that baseball returns to the New York Yankees and the New York Mets. May is Fleet Week when the West Side resembles a Navy dockyard and men and women in white uniforms are seen everywhere around the city. June brings with it the Puerto Rican Day parade with huge crowds and very loud music. July is Independence Day and the national fireworks that are also very loud. August is host to the U.S Open tennis tournament. September celebrates the Feast of San Gennaro in Little Italy. October ends with a spectacular Halloween parade in Greenwich Village. November has the nationally televised Macy's Thanksgiving Day parade, and December is tree lighting at the Rockefeller Center and The Nutcracker at the Lincoln Center.

It really is very hard to get bored in New York. Visitors come here for any one of the events listed above and the hundreds more not mentioned. Residents can take it for granted that so much is going on around them, but New Yorkers are normal folk who sometimes just need a night in, sitting in front of the television or reading a good book. My philosophy is that if you don't take part in anything that New York uniquely offers then there really is little point in living here. Whether you love it here or hate it, there is no arguing that this city has it all and then some more.

PART 5

Living in the City

CHAPTER 24

Making Friends in Manhattan

When I left England's shores to come to America, I left behind my immediate family and my closest friends. I began a new journey: meeting my wife, starting my own family, and the quest for new and lasting friendships. Making friends when you are older becomes more difficult and is made even harder by a severe change in location. The tendency is to stick to those people with whom you have the most in common and the expatriate community in Manhattan is large enough to enable newcomers to avoid the natives completely. By dating an American, I instantaneously was forced upon all of my future wife's friends' partners. It made not the slightest bit of difference if I had no shared interests or backgrounds with them. I had to spend many a night with men who equally dreaded seeing me. Over the years, some of these men have vanished from our social scene, due to breakups or lost contact or because I adamantly refused to see them by locking myself in the bathroom and not coming out until my wife agreed with me.

Over time, I have built up quite a selection of friends here in New York. I have my wife's friends' husbands, whom we see as foursomes. I have my wife's friends' husbands, whom I see independently outside of the foursomes. I have friends whom I see who have nothing to do with my wife, and I have work friends. Once friends leave the city and move to the suburbs, they might as well have moved to the moon. I honestly see my friends in England more than I see my once-closest friend who moved from around the corner out to Connecticut. He swore that we would see each other regularly once he moved, but between us we have seven children, so finding time to see one another is scarce, and I am not going up there: it's way too scary in Wilton for me. We have seen the same type of scenario with couples who have moved out. In the beginning, they make a huge effort to come to the city often and we always go and visit them at least once. Over time, the whole relationship fades unless both couples make a huge effort. It becomes a hassle to see them, and the thought of one couple sitting in traffic to get in or get out of the city means that visits are frowned upon.

Work friends become a much more convenient type of friendship. You see them every working day and share common interests that cover office politics and speaking about co-workers. It is also opportune to go out for a drink with them directly after work, and there is little pressure to see them outside of the office because you see them every day in the office. I have lots of work friends. I don't see them much on weekends because there is a separation between work and pleasure once Friday comes along. I also find that when you try to convert work friends into weekend friends, it usually becomes awkward and the wives don't get on and it affects the work friendship somewhat. Some stones are better off left unturned.

Most of my wife's friends are from her hometown in New Jersey, from her university, or are parents from our kids' school. We have no social friends in our building as we try to stay as anonymous as possible. We have no friends from my wife's previous workplace because she wasn't friendly with anyone when she worked there. We do see a few new friends because of our kids' friendships, and even though new friends are good and we will maintain these relationships for many years to come, we have very little shared history with them and I think it's fair to say that we are more peripheral friends to them than close friends.

It is hard to make really good friends in this city, as there is no real sense of community here. I am happy with this arrangement because it allows me to maintain a certain acceptable level of privacy and enjoy not having anyone knocking at my door and popping 'round unannounced. In Manhattan, you can be as friendly or as rude as you like and no one cares. You can talk to anyone in any restaurant or bar or you can sit on your own and not utter a single word to anyone. No one knows whether you are at home or not: there are no driveways to spot if cars are parked there and no one can peer into your windows to see if you are at home. And I love it, as when I come home from work and I open my apartment front door and walk in and close it behind me, I know I am not going to be bothered by anyone outside for the rest of the night. If anyone comes to see me from outside of my building, he has to be announced by the doorman and he has to call up and get permission from me, the tenant, to allow him access to the elevator. If I am not in the mood I simply don't answer the intercom. I can cocoon myself in my own apartment and my wife and I often do.

Singles also find Manhattan a difficult place to meet a lifetime partner in. Blind dates through Web sites and introductions are the most preferred methods to hook up with someone. Just because there are thousands of bars and nightclubs in the city, it doesn't mean these places are conducive to finding your true love and/or dream date. They are normally way too noisy and crowded and are populated with those who use bridges and tunnels to find entertainment away from their dreary and boring satellite towns. My wife and I, however, did meet in a bar in Manhattan, just to prove that it can happen. She is convinced it was a gay bar, as she went there after work with a friend to avoid being picked up by annoying, persistent men. I went there after work because I found out they serve a proper British pint of beer and that their selection of beers on tap was bigger than anywhere else I had seen so far in Manhattan. I did notice that ninety-nine percent of the clientele was male, but it never dawned on me that it wasn't a straight bar, and it didn't bother me either way. I was happy to have a nice pint with some work friends after we had clocked out for the day. Little did I know that my search for a decent pint would instead find me falling in love and forming an amazing relationship with the woman of my dreams. I have never been back to this bar since we met as I won't tempt fate. I don't need to be nostalgic, and if I go there by myself I will be accused by someone who would see me there of trying to stalk men, and if I go there with my wife she would accuse me of secretly having homosexual tendencies, so I can't win.

"How did you two meet?" is a common New York question. We tried to come up with an alternative version of how we met by making up a story that we were introduced by mutual friends. However, we never could come up with a credible tale as we both got stuck on the second question of who introduced us. People are shocked to hear that we met in a bar. Apparently it really isn't that common to meet in a bar, so I beg the question: If it doesn't happen, why do single people go to bars all the time in the hopes of finding a long-term partner?

People in New York City hook up with each other all the time, and single people love it here because it offers them so much choice and possibility. My single guy friends frequently visit hot spots to pick up women and take them home that night. They wouldn't want to marry the type of girl who would actually leave with them on their first meeting. My wife's single girlfriends also go to the same hot spots and go home with these men, but wouldn't want to marry a guy who frequents these types of places. Therefore, a fair number of people who frequent bars in New York City have a lot of fun, but stay single because they get caught up in the whole hypocrisy of their own situation. In reality, if they took a closer look at the hooking-up-at-bars issue, what they are really saying is they wouldn't want to marry themselves.

CHAPTER 25

The Weather

New York City used to have four distinct seasons. Spring and fall brought spectacular weather: not too hot and not too cold, but warm enough for just a T-shirt with temperatures in the midseventies. The street cafes would be amassed with people enjoying outdoor life and resemble European cities in the summer. Parks and playgrounds were crammed to capacity with families taking strolls in Central Park and biking around the six-mile loop. In the fall, the leaves on the trees in Central Park would change color, and any scene in a snapshot there would resemble some of the finest landscape paintings. During these two seasons, the city and its inhabitants were content, with street fairs and outdoor shows peppering the metropolis, inviting people to leave their abodes and wander outside to breathe in New York City life to its full.

I have no idea what changed, but it now seems like summer lasts for five months and winter for slightly more, leaving no time at all to enjoy spring and fall. It is like a global warming and a global cooling are pulling Manhattan twice a year in opposite directions.

The summers in the city are brutal. The humidity is so intense that even a short walk outside merits the need for a lengthy shower. The heat pounds the concrete sidewalks and asphalt roads and creates a haze as it rises and attempts to cook the pedestrians as they walk. Temperatures reach the high nineties for days on end, and even at night it doesn't cool off significantly for any meaningful relief. Without adequate air conditioning, you could pass out from suffocation as the hot air rises quickly through apartment buildings. In this hostile, scorching environment Manhattan feels like it is melting, with concrete lava spilling out in all directions, covering every nook and cranny of this island. The only escape is to meander into an office building or a shop where more powerful air conditioners suck dry the energy supply, heaving in gallons of hot, sticky air from outside and churning out what seems like ice-cold air back into the enclosed spaces.

Tempers are as heated as the weather, and patience wears thin on an exhausted, beaten-down population. Subway stations way below the surface act like ovens absorbing in the heat from all around and test the endurance of the most discerning of passengers. Reprieve is forthcoming once the train arrives as it provides incredible air conditioning to its riders. It pays to ride up and down the subway system in the depths of summer as these cooled-off cars offer one of the most effective ways of staying chilled during sweltering, oppressive August days. On summer weekends there is a mass exodus to the breezier coastlines of the Hamptons and the Jersey Shore and to homes in Connecticut and upstate New York, where swimming pools entice the overheated city dweller.

On the rare occasions when the weather is less intrusive over the summer weekends, Manhattan is a fabulous place to live. It is empty. Hard-to-come-by restaurant reservations open up, and the kids can take advantage of visiting the Central Park Zoo, the carousel, the boating lake, and walking around the neighborhood without being bowled over by the usual mass of people.

Wintertime is less oppressive but equally as difficult at times to move about in. New York City is not designed for heavy snowfalls, and with cold spells intermittent with rain and then freezing temperatures, icy conditions hit the city in a flash and make driving and walking fairly treacherous. The airports suffer tremendously in the winter when snow arrives. They just cannot cope with the sheer volume of traffic combined with subzero temperatures, and they back up immediately if there are signs of bad weather.

When it does snow, it is at first a beautiful scene. To walk in Central Park and sled down its hills when snow is fresh and still falling is reminiscent of any wintery picture postcard. My kids love nothing better than wrapping up warm and venturing out as soon as heavy snow starts falling. Hoards of people share similar pastimes and the parks are awash with families having fun frolicking in winter's delight.

The problem comes when the snow sticks around for a few days. The snow turns from white to grey to dark black very quickly, and when it starts melting, the drainage system on the roads gets blocked fairly fast. At intersections, where the pedestrian needs to cross major roads, deep puddles of water formed by the melting snow have turned to a color matching the asphalt, after having been polluted by the passing cars and buses. These immense puddles are very hard to see, especially at night, and a stray foot from the sidewalk onto the road disappears into a profound gathering of water that seeps into shoes and socks. The disgruntled person on foot steps back onto the sidewalk. As soon as they do, a taxi driver far too close to the side of the road uses the tires of his cab to spray the same dirty water onto the clothes of the misfortunate one, leaving the person wet all over, filthy, and most unhappy.

Snow has fallen in New York City as early as October 10 and as late as April 25, both witnessed in the late nineteenth century. The most snow in one day was in February 2006 when almost twenty-seven inches fell in a single twenty-four-hour period. The worst month for snowfalls is February. The most snow in one season was in 1995–96 when over seventy inches fell in the city in total. It sometimes feels like winter is here to stay in Manhattan, and temperatures with the wind chill stay at around zero for several consecutive days. It is particularly hard on the poorest sectors of our society, as choices are made between heating a home and food and medicine, and for the old who can't get out for fear of slipping on the ice.

Those who come to Manhattan to live don't come here for the weather, although I would argue that the extremes of both summer and winter in Manhattan beat the tornadoes of the Midwest and South, the hurricanes of the Deep South, the forest fires of California, and the number of rainy days in London.

CHAPTER 26

9/11 and Life After It

9/11 was quite simply the worst day ever in New York City's history, and coupled with the events in Washington DC and Pennsylvania, the biggest single death toll on American soil from acts of terrorism in a single day. Whenever I went to downtown, I always used the Twin Towers to find my bearings because the easy-to-follow grid system of streets runs out just north of downtown at First Street. If you looked one way and saw the Twin Towers, you knew you were facing the south. The void of the collapsed buildings is nothing compared to the emptiness felt by parents, partners, spouses, brothers, sisters, and children who lost loved ones who lived in the tristate area and beyond.

On the evening of September 10, I was at Yankee Stadium, sitting in the loge seats and waiting for a game against the despised Boston Red Sox. The rain never let up and the game was postponed. By the next morning, I noticed how the weather had changed so dramatically: it was a beautiful, sunny day with clear, crisp blue skies. I got up early as usual on that Tuesday morning, got dressed and left my apartment, walked the hallway to the elevator, and pressed the button to signal that I wanted to go down. The elevator never came. Both elevators were out of service. I walked the eight flights down with a gentleman who lived above me on a floor in the teens. We got to the lobby and walked to the corner of Eighty-fifth Street and Lexington Avenue. I didn't know his name. He didn't know mine either, but we chatted down the stairs and on the short walk to the street corner as acquaintances do. We bid farewell and wished each other a good day. I turned left to walk forty blocks to work in midtown to try to get a little exercise. He turned right to walk a block to the subway station to catch an express train downtown. I went to work and two hours later watched the television in shock as the events unfolded. He went to work and witnessed the whole horror and terror of it all and died somewhere between the 101st and 105th floor of One World Trade Center.

You walk left and live. You walk right and die. That is what I think of every time 9/11 is mentioned. I could have been working in that building. I had visited it several times on business, being employed in the financial service industry. I am one of the lucky ones.

How does a city recover from such an awful experience? How can we move on and be happy again? How do we stop feeling frightened and scared that another terrorist act is around the corner? How do we make New York City safer? How can we have fun again? Will New York City ever be the same again? These are the questions we all asked ourselves after 9/11.

And look at how amazing New York City is. It is the most resilient of places. It fights back. It refuses to lie down and die. It honors its fallen heroes and turns itself into an even better place. It decides to cleanse itself of its arrogance and be a friendlier place. It rebuilds, and it makes sure that it keeps itself on the podium for the greatest city in the world with the most resourceful and extraordinary people. It was injured. It was hurt. It was attacked. And it prevailed.

CHAPTER 27

The Two Blackouts

There are many different ways to measure how a city is fairing and to see changes over time. Economic statistics in New York City exist for measuring the unemployment rate, the average cost of housing, the average income per household, and various cost of living indices. Every ten years a national census is conducted that adds information about the size of the population in Manhattan, its ethnicity, and the number of people per household. Putting all these numbers together presents a clear picture of how many people live here, how wealthy the population is, and what the ethnic makeup of the city is. These numbers are immensely important for the allocation of funds and help urban planners improve services and channel resources into neighborhoods that need them most.

A third set of statistics informs the public of how safe the city is. On December 29, 2009, the New York Police Department (NYPD) announced that the city of New York had the least number of annual murders in forty-six years and that other major crimes were dramatically down too. This is particularly good news as during previous economic downturns crime in NYC has risen.

Statistics help formulate policy and establish trends, enable comparisons with other cities to be made, as well as track economic fluctuations. What they don't do is capture the vibe, the feel-good factors, the ambiance of NYC, or the way people behave. Anyone who has lived in Manhattan for over forty years will tell you that this city has improved beyond recognition, especially in the past fifteen years. It is cleaner, safer, more gentrified, has better facilities, has a superior police force, is better governed, and is much less corrupt than it used to be. Economic booms in the nineties and the beginning of the twenty-first century have contributed to these improvements, and the no-tolerance policy of law enforcement agencies in tackling crime and cleaning up previous no-go areas went hand in hand to ameliorate the quality of life of Manhattan residents. I am positive that drugs, prostitution, and extortion are still major problems in the city, but they have been taken away from the daily public eye and off the streets.

After dark, when the kids are in bed, my wife will often go out with her girlfriends for dinner or she will flip-flop over to the nail salon for a dose of pampering and some R and R. I worry about many things, but my wife's safety in our neighborhood is not one of them. She isn't walking the streets at three o'clock in the morning and hanging around dark passageways inviting trouble. She passes twenty-four-hour doormen buildings on our block and then turns onto a busy avenue with both pedestrian and vehicle traffic. I would worry about her more if she were walking to her car in a parking lot alone in the suburbs.

An excellent way of monitoring the temperament of NYC is to compare two almost identical events that occurred sixteen years apart and see how its population reacted to them differently. Two major blackouts knocked out New York City's power for one day during the summers of 1977 and 2003. They both lasted for around twenty-four hours until power was restored to most of the city. They both took place when temperatures were high, the first in July and the other in August.

In 1977 the city was deemed to be in economic decline with its coffers empty, crime was rampant and people were reeling after the Summer of Sam murders. Tensions were high. New York City's population was on the decline, and many of its buildings were vacant and boarded-up. Almost as soon as the lights went out on July 13, rioting and looting started on a grand scale in its poorest neighborhoods, costing the city hundreds of millions of dollars that it could ill afford to lose. The police eventually restored order, but the reputational damage was irreparable, as video and photos of the lawlessness were broadcast worldwide.

Contrast this with the events of 2003. In the late afternoon of August 14, New York City lost its power. Traffic signals switched off, elevators stopped working, and lights went out. I remember it well. I walked home from work. My mother had just landed at JFK airport from England and was trying to get into Manhattan. One of my kids was at summer day camp in Chelsea, and it took her four hours to get back to our neighborhood. I was dreading the oncoming nightfall, expecting the worst because of what I had read about the events of 1977. I was sent by my wife to the supermarket to stock up on bottled water and easy-to-eat canned food. There was no running water in a large number of apartment buildings because the water pumping system that takes water to the water towers at the top and then distributes it to each apartment is powered by electricity.

The supermarkets were packed with similar-thinking folk, and the lines to check out were enormous because the credit card payment machines were electrically operated and the cash registers couldn't open either. Eventually a manager stepped in and started taking cash, asking for correct change and using a battery-operated calculator to tally up the cost of the provisions. It seemed like wartime. Old-timers spoke of 1977 and warned newcomers to stay indoors when it turned dark. I walked up the eight flights of stairs from the lobby back to my apartment with heavy bags, and while panting for breath informed everyone, including the children, that we needed to batten down the hatches and hide under the beds because a full-scale riot was about to erupt.

The kids were hysterical, running around the apartment screaming and crying, and my wife told them not to take any notice of their father as the lack of power had affected his brain waves and his ability to think straight. Things did not look good. My mother was missing in action, most likely robbed by her taxi driver, and my eldest child was on a camp bus, stuck in traffic in midtown trying to get back home, and had probably passed out because of the heat and lack of liquid intake.

Then it got dark. I peered out from under the bed and crawled on all fours over to the window. I slowly pulled myself up to the ledge and afforded a quick glance to see what was going on in the jungle outside. Candles were flickering in other apartments, and on the streets parties were starting, with stoops full of people singing and clapping while eating and drinking. The crowds were high-fiving law enforcement officers as they walked past with flashlights, and store owners were standing outside of their convenience stores handing out beer, milk, and sodas. There was no price-gouging, no rioting, and no lawlessness. All I could see were ordinary people making the most of a bad situation.

So I went downstairs to wait for mother and child. When they arrived separately, they told me that total strangers had been giving them free food and drink along the whole route home and that parties were breaking out everywhere. These parties continued late into the night, and the only time I lost my temper throughout this whole ordeal was at one o'clock in the morning when someone playing guitar to his neighbors on a porch opposite started singing "Hey Jude" by the Beatles for the third time that night. I leaned out the window and screamed for him to play something else, but I was heckled and drowned out by a crescendo of the chorus.

This was no 1977. Crime levels were lower during this twenty-four-hour period than normal. The next day, when power was gradually restored, New Yorkers gave themselves a large pat on the back in honor of their achievement of creating a neighborly and safe place to live.

CHAPTER 28

Hatch, Match, and Dispatch

Getting Sick in New York

New York City hospitals are some of the world's finest. They attract patients from far-flung places because they provide the most modern and innovative medical techniques, engineered and administered by top-class medical staff. They are able to do this because the hospitals here are well funded by patient fees and also by generous benefactors who support all areas of medical science and whose contributions keep New York hospitals one step ahead of the competition. Every wing, building, operating theater, and room is named after somebody. When they run out of wall and door space and plaques, they will start engraving the names of donors on medical instruments. Doctors will start using the Davis Family Stethoscope and the Stevens Memorial Scalpel.

Whenever any of my family has been unwell on a trip outside of the city limits, I immediately seek local medical attention and then on return see a New York doctor to confirm what is really wrong with one of us. Both my daughter and I have been misdiagnosed in accidents we have had in other parts of the United States. Our family slogan is "In New York doctors we trust." There are so many doctors in New York City that there isn't enough room to house them all in the hospitals. Instead, doctors' offices occupy nearly all the ground floors of doormen buildings. The medical profession supplies the city with thousands of jobs. At every doctor's office there is a receptionist and someone who deals directly with the insurance companies as well as doctors' assistants. There are hundreds of pharmaceutical reps who cruise the city handing out samples to the doctors, trying to promote the newest and most effective drugs. Hospitals employ thousands of people, including doctors and nurses and technicians and administrative staff. The medical profession is a huge business and moneymaker for New York City.

Sometimes it feels like New York City is full of hypochondriacs. In a quest to stay healthy, many of the inhabitants here have multiple doctors covering every symptom and ache and pain they feel. The names and reputations of doctors are openly discussed at dinner parties, and having top-rate doctors is part of the social status quo of living here. I have heard people under forty speak about an entire inventory of doctors they frequent, even though they consider themselves healthy. This list includes general practitioners, internal medicine doctors, dermatologists, orthopedic specialists, psychiatrists, cardiologists, and brain surgeons. Listening to these people you would think they were near death considering the amount of appointments they go to. New Yorkers just don't take chances with their health, and if the best medical help is right here on their doorstep, they might as well utilize it.

I have a general practitioner whose name I fill in at the top of the form every time I go to his practice on the Upper East Side. I visit this office twice a year, once for my annual checkup and once because I need antibiotics, usually for strep throat. I haven't actually seen my doctor in six years. I always see one of the other nonpartner doctors in his practice or an assistant. The other day when I was there, I asked if I could make an appointment to see my main doctor and was told that the next available appointment was in six months. The receptionist then asked me what the appointment was about so that she could write it down in the notes. I stood there for a while thinking it didn't matter what it was about as I could be dead from a whole series of diseases I might catch on my travels in the next half year. I told her not to bother.

Giving Birth

Hopefully most of us don't really need to use the excellent doctors and hospitals here for a very long time. The only happy reason to visit a hospital is if you and your partner are having a baby. Manhattan hospitals are renowned for having the very best facilities for maternity care for both the mothers and the babies. I can vouch for this as three of my kids were born here. Once the child bearer has chosen an OBGYN affiliated with a particular hospital, a tour of the maternity floor is offered. It is a little bit like the private school application process, the difference being if you pay, you get in. The real reason for the tour is so that you know where to come to on the big day instead of wandering around other floors of the hospital, disturbing the sick and those providing health care to them.

The OBGYN will stress the first time around that you should not come to the hospital the moment the mother starts having contractions unless of course there are complications. The maternity wards only have a certain number of beds. If you arrive there too early you will be sent away. This happened to us the first time around. We didn't want to go home again, so we negotiated to leave my wife's suitcase at the hospital while we went for a walk outside. We were told to time the contractions and when they were a lot closer to come back for delivery. My wife had labor pains in her back. They are the most painful type and ones that cause the mother to become violent as a direct consequence.

We left the hospital and waddled over to a nearby convenience store to purchase some gummy bears and some bottles of water. As soon as we left the store a contraction occurred that caused my wife to double over in pain. I had been taught in our prenatal classes to gently rub her back, which I proceeded to do. In her minute of pain the only thing she could focus on was to clench her fist tightly and whack me really hard in the stomach while cursing. Passersby gave us a very wide berth. I can only imagine what this scene looked like to an outsider: a very pregnant woman screaming in pain, throwing out body punches at the person with her, and swearing like a trooper. I was winded in the stomach a couple of times but couldn't complain or react at all because my wife gave me a look as if to say "that is nothing compared to child birth and prelabor."

A couple of hours later we were back in the hospital, well on the way to meeting our new child. The epidural had been administered and so the husband-beating had stopped. My wife turned to me and said, "Don't forget: the second the baby is born you have to run downstairs to the cashier and make sure you get me a private room. You can hold the baby when you get back. You have to get me a private room. Do you understand?" Hospitals in the city, like its inhabitants, have limited space to operate in. There aren't enough single rooms in the maternity ward, and several mothers, after having gone through childbirth, have to share a room. In order to encourage sharing, they make the cost of a single room more expensive than a night in a suite at the Four Seasons Hotel. The private rooms are given out to those who want them after payment on a first-come, first-served basis. If there aren't any available, there is nothing you can do. Those that can't afford this luxury or who simply don't care are automatically transferred after birth into shared accommodation. Apparently my wife didn't fit into either of these categories, and I actually agreed with her. I thought it was worth spending the extra money on.

With my wife resting before the final push, I decided to do some reconnaissance work to find out our chances of getting a private room. There were six of them, and I ascertained from the names by the sides of the doors that four were occupied. There were three women in labor in the delivery rooms, and one couple looked like they were about to be sent away for being too early. Providing we gave birth first or second, I assumed there shouldn't be a problem. Then suddenly there was a lot of activity at the end of the hallway, with doors opening and closing and a lot of running by nurses and paging over the public announcement system about delivery room two. After a couple of minutes of frantic action, I heard crying from a newborn. I smiled for a second thinking I was so happy for the parents of this newborn, and then it suddenly dawned on me: our chances of a private room had just gone fifty-fifty. I went back to my wife and woke her up by tapping her on the shoulder. She was a little disorientated. I didn't want to tell her my worrying news, so instead I asked her if she could hurry it up a bit. That didn't go over too well. I could still hear the obscenities whizzing past my head as I left the delivery room again and went back into the hallway.

I thought long and hard about what I could do. You couldn't go downstairs to the cashier's office and prebook the room, as you needed the delivery slip from the doctor. Therefore, the only thing to do was to find the father of my competitor and try to persuade him of the merits of shared accommodation and talk about how disgustingly expensive the room charge was for a private room. I thought I had found him in the waiting room and proceeded to preach to him about sharing and saving money. He totally agreed with me. The only problem was he turned out to be the boyfriend of one of the nurses who had come to the hospital to pick her up after her shift had ended.

While I continued to look for the other father-to-be, my wife had started the final push and I was nowhere to be found. I debated going into the other delivery room and just asking the mother if she was intending to purchase a private room. Just as I was about to knock on the door, I heard a loudspeaker announcement asking for a Rob Silverman to come immediately to the delivery room where my wife was. I arrived about three minutes before our beautiful daughter was born. The second she came out, I sprinted for the elevator and then turned around quickly back to the room to get the correct paperwork from the doctor. I was a mess. I had won the competition for the private room, and as I handed the credit card over to the cashier I pumped my fist in the air in victory.

Marriage and Divorce

There is something dreamy about getting married in New York City. There are so many photo opportunities for backdrops to wedding pictures, like taking in a Manhattan skyline or a lush floral scene in Central Park. There are also many different venues to hold the ceremony and reception in. There are beautiful religious institutions covering all denominations as well as stunning hotels and reception halls. The cost of holding a status-symbol Manhattan wedding is astronomical. The hiring of the hall, the food, the wine, the flowers, and the photography are all more expensive than comparable out-of-town soirees. A wedding in the city can cost in the hundreds of thousands of dollars.

Divorces are equally as expensive. Top New York divorce attorneys charge almost $1,000 an hour, and a discourteous divorce with children involved can cost as much as the wedding that put the two feuding parties together. New York City, like many other places, is home to many who are on their second or third marriages. Blended families are becoming just as much he norm than conventional ones. Same-sex partners are an equal part of New York society, as are interfaith and interracial relationships. Judging someone else for an alternative lifestyle is ludicrous when you live in a giant melting pot. There is no accepted norm here like in the suburbs. New Yorkers are different in their backgrounds, in their culture, and in their behavior. It is exactly this type of tolerance that attracts the liberal, carefree, mind-your-own-business type of world citizen and what gives New York its reputation for being a city where anything and everything goes.

Burials

New York City is one of the most expensive cities in the world. Entertainment, business, and shopping epicenters are located in Manhattan. Millions of people come here every day to work, shop, and have fun. It is accessible by boat, by helicopter, by rail, by foot, and by car. Its residents are immersed in a sea of culture with an enormous choice of restaurants, and the city serves as a template for convenience-style living. Most things can be done in Manhattan. You can trapeze in Battery Park, play indoor tennis in a bubble underneath the Fifty-ninth Street Bridge, get lost in the Ramble in Central Park, and spend hours gazing at the exhibits in the newly renovated Museum of Modern Art in midtown.

The only thing you can't do in Manhattan, no matter how much money you have: get buried here. There just isn't space for the dead. Apart from a few eighteenth-century Dutchmen buried in the church graveyards downtown, everyone else gets carted out. If your faith allows cremation, then your ashes can be sprinkled on the lawns of Central Park or on the sidewalks of Wall Street, but if you want to return your body to the soil, then the outer boroughs or suburbs is the only way. This is why when I am asked if I intend on staying in Manhattan, I always answer yes and add that the only way I would leave this city is in a box six-feet long with nails in it. I want to spend the rest of my life here and would compromise my lifestyle to stay if it became unaffordable, but even I know there are restrictions, and that I can't be here for eternity.

CHAPTER 29

The Rich, the Poor, and Everyone Else

Property prices in Manhattan have skyrocketed, particularly in the last two decades. Those who bought early on are now sitting on ridiculous levels of equity in their apartments, even though the market peaked in 2007 and then fell 10 to 15 percent. According to a New York Times article, in October 2009 the average price of an apartment in Manhattan was $1.5 million. Obviously anyone buying an average apartment in 2010 has to be earning a decent wage and has considerable savings to boot. They have to be millionaires. New entrants buying into Manhattan real estate and those rich tenants already here come from all walks of life, but generally they are connected to either Wall Street, the medical profession, the legal field, the advertising world, the entertainment business, or big business.

The zip codes of 10021 and 10022 are the wealthiest zip codes in the country based on tax returns submitted to the IRS. These neighborhoods constitute the renowned Upper East Side and the Upper West

Side, which flank Central Park from Fifty-ninth Street all the way up to Seventy-ninth Street. They include such notorious rich avenues as Fifth, Madison, Park, and Central Park West. This affluent group of New Yorkers displays the wealth of the city extremely flamboyantly. Unlike in some other societies where wealth is frowned upon, in Manhattan it is flaunted. The size of some of the luxury apartments inside gloriously ordained buildings is simply mind-blowing. Open up a Wall Street Journal weekend edition at the property section and the sheer decadence and cost of these monstrosities in the sky will overwhelm most common folk. Chauffeurs line the avenues waiting for their employers to emerge from their palaces to drive them around the city to work, lunch, or shop.

New York's elite step out onto the sidewalks jeweled to the hilt, immaculately clothed, and in winter, wrapped in the most expensive furs money can buy. They wine and dine at the most exclusive restaurants; they are members of all the established and well-known private clubs and get groomed at the top hair salons, the best plastic surgeons, and outrageous spas. Most of the super rich spend colossal amounts of money on their appearance and will rarely step out into Manhattan unless they look the part. They never go grocery shopping, they have never visited a dry cleaner, they don't cook, they never do laundry, and they don't use public transportation. They are an enigma. They are an integral part of the social fabric of the city and no one bats an eyelid at them when they are out. New York City wouldn't be the same without them.

At the other extreme, almost 18 percent of the Manhattan population lives below the federal poverty line as recorded by the city, taken from income tax returns, and displayed on Wikipedia. The poor are also concentrated in certain geographical areas with many living in lower Manhattan. This is where you find many of the tenement buildings still dotted with apartments without self-contained bathrooms. The poorer residents are helped out in the form of rent controls and food stamps, and many charities look in on the elderly and infirmed.

New York City is a very different urban experience for those trapped in poverty, squalor, and despair. These folk rarely leave their neighborhoods. They are immersed in unemployment and rely on welfare for survival. Those who work find it very difficult to make ends meet because of the expense of living in the city, but are trapped since they can't afford the moving costs to exit to cheaper towns in the tristate area.

When you visit one of these buildings, you get a sense of the desperation and you can literally smell the poverty in the hallways. When I first arrived in New York a friend of mine took me to a building he partly owned on Seventh Street in the Lower East Side. The building was a walk-up and tenement in style with six stories. By the time I reached the top, I was out of breath and panting. My friend wanted me to visit an elderly woman in her nineties who was on rent control and spoke no English. She was a German immigrant, arriving in New York in the 1930s, and had lived in this studio apartment with a bathroom in the corridor shared by her neighbors ever since. It had never been renovated. We were visiting her to see if there was anything she needed so as to improve her living conditions, and I was brought along because I spoke German.

Her rent was $87 a month, and had steadily risen from $12 a month just after the war. She could barely afford her rent, medicines, and food. She had never married and had no children. Her siblings had already passed away and her living friends could no longer visit her because they couldn't climb the stairs. Neighbors did her shopping for her and she never ventured outside, only going to the bathroom once a day in fear of being attacked in the hallways, as that had happened six years before. My friend had only owned the building for a few months and genuinely wanted to help her. No previous landlord had ever had a conversation with her about apartment improvements because she paid the rent on time each month. She was the perfect rent-controlled tenant. She was one of the many in New York City who slip through the system. She represented the forgotten side of the city. There are thousands and thousands of them. This was the New York that visitors rarely come across and most New Yorkers try not to see.

We knocked on the door and waited, hearing shuffling noises coming from within. The door opened after a few minutes, and a little, hunched-up lady stood in the doorway, looking up at the two of us. She spoke in very broken English and ushered us into her tiny apartment. She knew we were coming, as my friend had notified her by mail and had told the superintendent to inform her as well. I started speaking to her in German and her face lit up. We had a very healthy and vibrant conversation about New York City and how I was able to speak German. She spoke of her love of her former homeland and how grateful she was for the United States for saving and supporting her.

The one thing I couldn't get out of my head was the smell. It was of previously cooked, stale food mixed with dampness and mold. The apartment wasn't clean either. Dust balls were everywhere, and bits of ancient food specimens were scattered on the floor, visible to the naked eye. The woman wasn't well taken care of either. She had cuts and burn marks on her arms and her hair was mangled and dirty. The whole scenario reeked of poverty. I turned to my friend and proprietor and asked him how he could help her so that I could translate. He offered a cleaning service, a new oven, new windows to keep the drafts out, and new radiators for improved heating efficiency. I told her of all these improvements and she thanked me profusely, but then declined them all. She told me she couldn't afford the rent increase. I again translated her fears back to my friend who told me that there would be no rent increase at all for any of the services and amenities that he was offering. When I reported back to her the good news, we were embraced tightly by this very affectionate and thankful elderly woman.

It felt good. We had done more for her in ten minutes than previous landlords had done in fifty years and we had made her day, if not her year. My friend informed me later that all the work had been done and this is how New Yorkers should be in their dealings with their tenants. The system allows my friend to take back the apartment when this woman passes on, as there is no one to inherit the rent-controlled property. The rent can then increase from $87 to $800. The difference between my friend and many other landlords is compassion. He didn't have to spend anything on her and would still take back the apartment on her death. The fact that he tried to make her life better in her later years should reap its rewards for him once this lady has moved on.

The most common visual display of poverty in New York City is the homeless. They are more abundant in Manhattan than in any other of the boroughs since they are more successful in getting handouts there. The number of shelters for the homeless varies, depending on the city budget and which administration is in power. Many of the homeless fear being in a shelter, where crime and abuse is high, and consider the street a safer place to live. Food programs for the homeless are scattered around the city, operated by charities and religious organizations, and at various times of the day lines can be seen forming by those who need real help outside food distribution centers. The homeless can earn small amounts of money by partaking in recycling initiatives, handing back cans and bottles to the supermarkets.

Having been in many cities worldwide, I would say that homelessness in Manhattan is no greater than in any other city, but this may be distorted by the fact that for many years in NYC the problems concerning real poverty have been brushed under the carpet. There has been a concerted effort in the past to take the homeless off the streets, but as the economy has deteriorated the numbers have begun to increase once more. What is clear in Manhattan is that poverty is widespread. Poverty is very difficult to escape from, and many of those below the poverty line know no other existence than squalor and reliance on others. They can't move out of the city because they have nowhere to go and cling on to the hope that one day their fortunes will change.

A few generations ago it was much easier to get ahead even if one was poor. Many of my wife's family lived in cramped, awful conditions down on the Lower East Side of Manhattan and worked their way out of poverty against all the odds, including language and cultural barriers. They all eventually moved away to the suburbs, following their American dream. This process is not as common today. Opportunities are scarcer to better oneself because of the decline in the mobility of labor, and unskilled jobs in the city have begun to disappear. Poverty may not be highly visible in the areas most New Yorkers live, work, and play in, and many New Yorkers turn a blind eye to it, but thousands participate and volunteer their time on a daily basis to improve the lives of those less fortunate than themselves, and this should be highly commended.

Everyone Else

The majority of those who live in New York fit somewhere in the middle of the wealth ladder. They are neither rich nor poor and consider themselves middle-class. This group of people is most susceptible to moving-out disease. They make ends meet by and large from paycheck to paycheck, and never really get ahead because the cost of living in Manhattan is so high. They all know in the back of their minds that their stay in New York City will be a fleeting one. They have already mapped out how long they will stay, where to move, and what type of improved living space they will strive for when doomsday comes.

This transient majority contributes to Manhattan society in huge ways. They fill rental apartment buildings, pay taxes to the city, keep the restaurants in business, put bottoms on seats in movie theatres, and keep the city busy, vibrant, and alive to name a few. Most are young and, in many cases, single or newlyweds. They lower the average age of the inhabitants of Manhattan considerably and add a youthful flavor to many a neighborhood where rents are more affordable on the Manhattan scale. They also differentiate themselves from the Bridge and Tunnel Crowd who flock to Manhattan for the nightlife Thursday to Saturday. The temporary Manhattan resident looks down on those who have remained in the suburbs and frowns upon their lack of adventure for failing to live up to the challenge of giving up the suburbs for a few years, expressing their youth before it's too late, and trying an urban life in Manhattan.

There is one more category of Manhattan residents that needs to be explored. I fit into this box quite perfectly. The most accurate description of this rare breed of person encompasses adjectives such as stubborn, unrealistic, and delusional. We are neither the super rich nor the poverty-stricken. We fit perfectly into the in-between crew, who should consider life outside the city because of the high cost of living here. We should want to give our children more living space and a backyard to run around in, but we choose not to. We should save more money by living a cheaper life in the suburbs, but it doesn't ever cross our minds. We stay in Manhattan, not because we can afford to do so and not because we can't move to the suburbs and live a happy life elsewhere. We are the obsessed. We simply have fallen in love with this city. We can't imagine not living here. We get frustrated with some of the inconveniences of Manhattan life, including the noise, the traffic, and the tourists but we stay. We leave the city to visit friends and family and have a wonderful time outside, but always look forward to coming back. We defend our way of life vigorously when confronted by suburbanites who don't even try to understand our point of view. We totally believe that we are living our life to its maximum potential and that our Manhattan way of life is far superior to any other on this planet.

My whole family left Manhattan on the Sunday of a holiday weekend to spend a night away from the city with friends who had recently moved to Connecticut. We were very much looking forward to seeing their new home and meeting their new friends and experiencing life outside of Manhattan so that in our forceful defense of our existence we had something to compare it to. We arrived just in time for lunch. Our friends had invited four other families with kids to join us. It was buffet-style. They lived within two streets of each other. The kids there went to the same school, the families arrived by car even though they all lived within walking distance, everyone had the same car, and all the families had bought the same stroller. My wife and I found this to be a little surreal.

The meal was fabulous. Lots of salads and fruits and desserts, and the hospitality displayed by the hosts was second to none. The conversation seemed to be focused on deviant couples living in their town and the latest tidbit of gossip concerning them. We had no idea whom they were talking about and didn't want to partake in rumors and hearsay. The conversation reached a complete frenzy when one particular couple was mentioned. They lived next door to our friends, and everyone seemed to have the same opinion about the wife and mother of this family. I made one comment about the anonymity of Manhattan and that I couldn't speak badly about any of our neighbors because I really didn't know anything about their lives. Their kids were different ages than ours and went to other schools in the neighborhood.

I was starting to get aggravated at the direction of the conversation of these otherwise very nice folk. It seemed that everyone knew everybody in town and all their intimate details too. They knew what they earned and what vacations they took, what additions were made to their houses, when they bought a new car, and what jobs they all had. I was horrified. Ask any non-board member in my building what I do for a living and he would reply, "Who?"

I could see that this overnight trip outside of

Manhattan could soon fall into the category of danger-
ous to my health and challenging to my core beliefs.
The suburbs are rife with gossipmongers and evil neighbors, giving reason for the chitchat. So right after lunch,
I took the car keys and walked alone outside and started
the car and repositioned it at the end of the driveway in
case I needed a quick getaway. I returned to the house
feeling much better since I now had an exit strategy. I
calculated that with Sunday-afternoon traffic, I could
be back in my apartment in two hours if events further
deteriorated. I walked into the dining room where everyone was seated and whispered into my wife's ear, "I
can't stay here tonight." She motioned for me to come
closer to her so that she could privately tell me something too and I obliged. "Let's leave now. I'll come up
with an excuse," she said to my relief. Suddenly my wife
got up and announced to everyone that she had to return to New York immediately because something serious has come up. She left the room and went to gather
the children.

Everyone's eyes were on me, and I did what I do
best in these situations. I shrugged my shoulders and
told my newly formed audience that I had no idea what
was going on. Someone asked me if he was blocking me
in the driveway, but I responded that this wasn't a problem since, although we were the first guests to arrive,
our car was positioned right at the end of the driveway
so that we could get out. This remark was one of the
best conversation stoppers I have ever witnessed, as it
dawned on everyone there that my escape was premedi-
tated. Within five minutes, all our overnight belongings

were back in the car, including the kids, our farewells and nice-to-meet-yous had been said, and we were hurtling back toward our comfort zone. Our trip to the suburbs had been brief.

We still visit all our suburban friends but never accept overnight invitations as we can't be away from Manhattan for a single night, knowing that we can make it back by simply driving home.

CHAPTER 30

Where Are You From?

One of the most common questions New Yorkers ask one another is, "Where are you from?" I usually cause havoc in answering this question, as my response is normally, "The Upper East Side of Manhattan." The one asking then retorts with, "Where were you from before that?" and to this question I answer, "The Upper West Side of Manhattan." This is technically true as I made the switch after living in Manhattan for a year.

What people really want to know is where you were born, when you came to America, and how long you have lived in New York City. The question "Where are you from?" is so vague and meaningless, but everyone asks it, including me. It's a part of New York City speech. We ask it to everyone, including taxi drivers, nannies, teachers, superintendants, nail salon workers, hair stylists, friends, and we even ask dates this question on the first night. It is a great conversation starter. However, it is a politically incorrect question as I found out when training at my last firm for interviewing graduates.

You can't ask someone in an interview where he is from as the answer can lead to discrimination and lawsuits. Example: "He asked me where I was from. I said I was from Iran. The interview came to an abrupt halt and I didn't get the job." You see where this is leading. The best policy when interviewing is not to ask anything unrelated to the job. You can't even ask where the candidate came from the morning of the interview, never mind where he originally came from, as it has nothing to do with his suitability for the job in question.

The real issue of "Where are you from?" stems from the fact that many in New York were not born here. From the 1950s until the 1980s, Manhattan's population was on the decline. As wealth per capita increased, the American dream portrayed home ownership as the best expression of the fulfillment of that dream. Most folk in Manhattan rented and couldn't realize that dream in the city. Crime levels also started to rise, and Manhattan became a symbol of everything that was wrong with the inner cities. Parts of Harlem became no-go areas, Times Square was overrun by the sex industry and its workers, and buildings remained unrented and boarded up all over the city. Manhattan was deteriorating.

Manhattan started to turn around again in the 1980s and 1990s as prosperity returned. New high rises were built that housed more people, and the population began increasing again. Many of the Manhattan population who fled during the barren years to the safer existence of the suburbs have now returned, rekindling the Manhattan spirit that was missing for decades. In the past twenty years, the pace of property inflation in

Manhattan has outstripped that of any other part of the United States. Manhattan has become unaffordable for the masses. It is still a Mecca for the young and those who want to be entertained, and so we witness a somewhat transient population. The young professionals rent here in droves. When they start earning decent salaries and bonuses, they upgrade from studios and shared accommodations to renting or owning their own apartments. When they meet their better halves they stay in the city until the first child is born, and when number two is on the way, space becomes an issue, as does the cost of the private schools, and a huge exodus occurs to the satellite towns in the tristate area. The ones left behind in Manhattan are the very rich; the very poor, who can't move because they are subsidized and the moving costs are too high; and the stubborn like myself who won't commute, won't live in a cookie-cutter house, and who just love it here so much that they get all tingly inside whenever a move to the suburbs is mentioned.

The result of all this moving in and moving out is that there are few who can say they are true New Yorkers who have lived here their whole lives. This rare breed was born here, was schooled here, and since college graduation has lived and worked here. Others pretend to be this kind of New Yorker, and after delving into their past one finds out they are guilty of their own insanity. They have convinced themselves that they have always been here even though they were neither born here nor lived the majority of their life here.

The most amusing of this breed are the ones who travel abroad on vacation and tell people when asked that they come from New York City. Embarrassing them with a whole host of questions to expose their real domiciles is one of my specialties, since my English accent throws them off completely. I tend to mind my own business when I am away on vacation and enjoy my valuable catch-up time with my wife and children. I spend the first few days getting used to not being in Manhattan and the last few days yearning to return. The couple of days sandwiched in between are usually quite relaxing. The places I visit are normally in Europe, and the hotels are frequented by a whole array of different nationalities. Since there are about three hundred million Americans and they have large amounts of disposable income, it is common practice to find many in the hotels I stay in. My wife is originally from New Jersey, and she has a very similar accent to the nondescript Manhattan accent that my kids speak with.

You can definitely tell the difference between the bland Manhattan tongue and the quite distinctive Long Island drawl and the Brooklyn pronunciation of such words as "dawg" (dog) and "cawfee" (coffee). Hanging around a family with New York City accents while blurting out the Queen's English that is from across the pond and not the Fifty-ninth Street bridge version attracts quite a lot of attention from other Americans. Europeans don't care where you are from. They don't differentiate between those from California and New York, nor do they care if you are Belgian or Dutch. The European vacationers also keep to themselves and rarely strike up conversation at the pool or at lunch.

I remember being on the Riviera with my family

and a rather loud, middle-aged couple without children. They happened to be in the swimming pool at the same time as me. I was frolicking around with the kids, playing silly swimming games and generally having a fantastic morning enjoying my family in the sun and not thinking about work. I stopped playing for a few moments when my kids dived underwater and saw the husband of this middle-aged couple nod to me, and then he started moving closer to me.

"I am Richard Davidson," he announced, with his hand outstretched just above the water line. "Your kids are adorable." I of course thanked him for the compliment and turned away to turn my attention to my kids who were calling out to me.

"Where are you from?" he interjected quickly. Oh dear, I thought. Here we go again. Always the question where are you from. So I turned around to face him. "I'm from London," I said, pausing for him to take in the information and digest. I then added after a while, "Originally." I refused to play the game of asking him where he was from and was getting irritated that he was taking me away from my kids. But Mr. Davidson wanted to tell me where he was from. I sort of kept him hanging there, as it is common etiquette to reciprocate in this line of questioning. He didn't wait for me to ask since he sensed that I wasn't interested in him or his address.

"I am from New York," he blurted out, and this immediately grabbed my attention. So I turned around and engaged him. I asked him where in New York and he came back answering my question with the question of, "Do you know it well?" "Yes," I said, "quite well."

"I am from New York City," he said, arousing my interest further.

"Where in the city?"

"The town of Roslyn," he said. "Have you heard of it? Probably not. It's in New York City."

I could have so much fun with this guy, I thought. So I paused for a second and started my minitirade.

"It is very nice to meet you, Mr. Davidson. Roslyn, Long Island, is at exit 37 on the Long Island Expressway, some thirty-odd miles from Manhattan. It is not in New York City, sir. It is in Nassau County in New York State. I live in New York City, and before you interrupt me, which I can see you are about to do because your mouth is wide open, I live in the actual city, the Upper East Side of Manhattan. You asked me where I was from. I answered "London" because I have an accent and that is where I grew up and I generally don't give out my life story to strangers. You didn't ask me where I live because I would have told you the truth, that being New York City; Manhattan; New York, New York. I can say it twice because that is correct. You can only say it once.

He was dumbfounded and speechless. He had no comeback at all. I obviously had overreacted completely to this friendly but forward individual, but I was aggravated by all the New York City imposters that I kept meeting when I was away on vacation and took out my frustration on him.

It is amazing the draw of the city makes people believe that they actually live there. The boundaries of New York City in the eyes of many extend far beyond the five boroughs, which is the correct NYC definition. Pretenders claimed to live in New York City as far away as south New Jersey and Connecticut. Anyone from the tristate area traveling abroad claims to be from NYC and rarely does anyone challenge him or her as to the legitimacy of this assertion.

The real question here is: Who is a New Yorker? I have lived in Manhattan for thirteen years, but to most other New Yorkers I am as much a pretender as all the other phonies. My accent doesn't help me. I am proud of my origins and love the fact that I was born and raised in England. I am equally as proud and defensive of my newly adopted home city. I will always be labeled an Englishman and a Londoner, and no matter how hard I try or wish for it, I will never be considered a real New Yorker. The real ones also refer to my wife as a Jersey girl because she only moved to New York City in her twenties as well.

My kids are New Yorkers and will always be so as long as they don't engage in mutiny and move out when they get older. I could live here until my death (hopefully at a ripe old age) and still never be considered one of them. It really doesn't bother me that I can't obtain membership to such an exclusive club, but I'm glad that I can get a permanent visitor's card and still benefit from everything that members experience too.

At one of my previous jobs, I sat at a desk with twenty people in a trading room of approximately three hundred employees. Of the twenty on the desk, including myself, two were born in Manhattan, and of those two only one lived here. So taking a reasonable sample and applying it to the whole city, only 5 percent of those in Manhattan are real New Yorkers. So in essence, it really doesn't matter that I am not a true New Yorker. I am still welcome here and can live side by side with the real ones without any conflict. The only thing I can't do is hold my head up high and tell them that I am as much of a New Yorker as they are because they then become very defensive and infuriated.

About the Author

Rob Silverman was born in 1968 in Birmingham, England. He was educated in London, graduating University College London with a BS in economics and economic history. Rob moved to Manhattan in 1996, where he lives now with his wife, Janet, and their four kids, Jonah, Marlee, Bradley, and Dana, and became an American citizen in 2005. Rob works in finance, and is the author of *The Job Lottery: A Graduate's Guide to Getting a Job*, which was published by Smaller Sky Books in 2002 in the UK and US.